Contents

Cover: Soviet glorification of Lenin's arrival in Russia, April 1917
Front endpaper: Krupskaya—Lenin's wife—addresses Red troops during the civil war, 1918
Rear endpaper: Lenin and his successor, Stalin—the colleague whom he most distrusted

Copyright © 1971: G. Katkov and H. Shukman
First published 1971 by Macdonald
St Giles House 49 Poland St London W1
in the British Commonwealth and
American Heritage Press
551 Fifth Avenue New York NY 10017
in the United States of America
Library of Congress Catalogue
Card Number: 77-170176
Made and printed in Great Britain by
Purnell & Sons Ltd Paulton Somerset

LENIN'S PATH TO POWER

Bolshevism and the Destiny of Russia

George Katkov/Harold Shukman

Library of the 20th Century
Macdonald/American Heritage

Introduction
The Legend

In 1923 the Soviet writer M. Koltsov remarked: 'How strange that we so admire him, so love him, and yet know him personally so little . . . The living Lenin is even now totally unknown and incomprehensible to us.'

Not very much has changed since that time, either in the glorification of, or in our information about, Lenin. We still know little of certain basic facts of Lenin's personal and political life in spite of the enormous amount of literature on it and the vast efforts spent by researchers both in the Soviet Union and elsewhere on elucidating minute and irrelevant details of the man's life and activities. One might expect that those who consider him almost superhuman would have shown interest in the genealogy of their hero, but except for a few conventional remarks about his parents by his brothers and sisters and a cousin, there is hardly any account of his earlier ancestry. Similarly, the years during which the character of Vladimir Ulyanov (Lenin's real name) was formed seem to be covered only by the memoirs of his sisters, while the lively reminiscences of his schooldays recorded by a schoolmate who shared a desk with Lenin for six consecutive years have been ignored by most of his biographers.

Most biographies also fail to account for the environment in which Lenin grew up on Kokushkino, the estate of his maternal grandfather in the Samara province. More disturbing are the confused attempts by Lenin's biographers at describing his motives for joining the revolutionary movement. Was it the personal influence of his elder brother Alexander, who was hanged for his part in a plot to assassinate the Tsar Alexander III when Vladimir was sixteen? Was it his early reading of Russian revolutionary literature and of the first translations of Marx that led the young Vladimir onto the path towards the violent overthrow of the existing order? And precisely when did Lenin become conscious of belonging to the revolutionary movement? All this remains, to a large

Left: The image of the hero — Lenin, least vain yet most idolised of dictators, captivates the crowd in Red Square, 1919

extent, unclear or is obfuscated by political bias and legend-mongering. Lenin himself was remarkably secretive, especially about his personal life, and his rare and sparse remarks are of little help in answering these questions.

For the rest of his life we possess an invaluable source in the five successive editions of his writings, as well as in the occasional letters which are from time to time published in the Soviet Union, and sometimes outside it. These writings have become the sacred text whose authority has been invoked for justifying and extolling the sometimes very different and even contradictory policies of world Communism. In using this material we should, of course, remember that most of Lenin's writings were political pamphlets aimed at a given, fleeting, political situation where theoretical expositions are constantly interspersed with sharp and vitriolic polemics mainly directed against fellow revolutionaries who, in his eyes, had deviated from or betrayed the cause of the Revolution. Lenin's works are highly important, however, for an understanding of political developments after Lenin seized power. It is no less important to remember that hardly anything that Lenin wrote would have survived had he died before 1917. His writings and activities would then have appeared to be relevant only to the 'lunatic fringe' of the Russian revolutionary movement.

From 1900 to 1917, with one brief interval of 1905-7, Lenin spent his life outside Russia, and his impact on Russian political and social life during that period was negligible. Since his victory in 1917, the history of Russia in the preceding years of the century has, for many historians, been superseded by the history of the revolutionary movement. If, however, historical analysis has been able to disentangle the minute convolutions inside Lenin's infinitesimal revolutionary clan in the period 1900 to 1914, the situation becomes ever more confusing with the outbreak of the First World War. What organisational structure Lenin had managed to build up and maintain then collapsed completely. He was also dismayed by the breakdown in 1914 of the international socialist organisation, known as the Second International, which had pledged itself to prevent wars. Internationalist principles weakened when the parliaments of Europe voted on war credits.

The years 1914-17 were ones of unprecedented **10** ▷

*Right: Posters proclaim the slogans of the Soviet regime. 'Communism is Soviet power plus electrification' **(top left)**; 'Let the upper classes tremble at the approach of Communism!' **(top right)**; Marx and Lenin show the way to the working classes of the world **(bottom)**. **Next page:** Lenin personally portrayed directing the course of the October Revolution*

ФИКАЦИЯ

...ОЙ ДАЕШЬ ТОК!

...ИЗМ ЭТО

...ЛЕКТРОФИКАЦИЯ

ПУСТЬ ГОСПОДСТВУЮЩИЕ КЛАССЫ СОДРО-
ГАЮТСЯ ПЕРЕД КОММУНИСТИЧЕСКОЙ
РЕВОЛЮЦИЕЙ

1917   1922

ГЛАВНЫЙ ДОКЛАДЧИК   4го КОНГРЕССА О
ПЯТИЛЕТИИ   РЕВОЛЮЦИИ

МАРКСИЗМ-ЛЕНИНИЗМ
ПУТЕВОДНАЯ ЗВЕЗДА
РАБОЧЕГО КЛАССА
И ТРУДЯЩИХСЯ
ВСЕГО МИРА!

tension for Lenin. They are also years which present his biographer with a particularly difficult task. The temptation to use the opportunities which only war could offer to the revolutionary movement must have been overwhelming. We now know what use Lenin did, in fact, make of these opportunities. But owing to the systematic misinformation which led Lenin's biographers to ignore his involvement with the German government, it took almost forty years to find out the truth.

We are luckier as far as sources are concerned for the period during and after the Bolshevik seizure of power. There is a considerable amount of contemporary material explaining the leading part which Lenin played in the events of that time. Two factors demand that such sources should be approached with caution. First, this material contains much naive, unenlightened, and often insincere hero-worship (as, for instance, in the American John Reed's account in *Ten Days that Shook the World*). Secondly, there is a calculated distortion of what actually happened both by Soviet historians and to a much lesser extent by their colleagues in the West. Many people who alongside Lenin played a major part in the revolution have in the meantime become 'unpersons', leaving a vacuum into which historians have allowed Lenin's personality to bulge, expanding its qualities, exceptional by any standard, to the dimensions of a colossus.

The end of Lenin's political activities and earthly life is similarly concealed from our sight by a screen of official misinformation and suppression of facts. We do not know for sure what the terrible disease was which first struck Lenin in late 1921 and then reduced him to a vegetable-like existence for the last eleven months of his life. Whatever it might have been, we are entitled to ask how far back the deterioration of his mental activity began before the state of his brain made speech and purposeful movement impossible for him.

A mystery related to this is the nature of his conflict with some of his followers in the last months of his political activity, and in particular with the man who was to become his successor. Not even Khrushchev's revelations in his most famous speech in 1956 (ironically referred to as secret) explain fully the character and origins of this conflict. For decades it was glossed over by Stalin himself, beginning with his funeral oration in which he swore a solemn oath not to depart from Lenin's path and ending with the cult of Lenin's personality which was to become the mould from which the cult of Stalin's own personality — 'the Lenin of our days' — was to be cast.

Right: Manufacturing Soviet myths — a sculptor's workshop crowded with members of the changing Communist pantheon

Chapter 1
Young Lenin

Lenin, or to give him his proper name, Vladimir Ulyanov, the second son of Ilya and Maria Ulyanov, was born in the town of Simbirsk on the Volga on 10th April 1870. His father was at that time an inspector of elementary schools in the Simbirsk province. This was a government post and Lenin's father had had a remarkable career in this field, typical in the period of expansion and social mobility following the great reforms of Alexander II. Coming from the poorest stratum of the population of a distant provincial town, Astrakhan, obviously with a Tartar or Kalmyk ancestry, Lenin's father made good first as a teacher of mathematics, then as an administrator of secondary schools. In their memoirs his daughters remember him as a quiet man, completely dedicated to his official work and his family. Lenin's schoolmate, Alexander Naumov, remembers him as a small old man of the unctuous type: short, thin, with a sparse greying beard, dressed in the frock-coat uniform of the Ministry of Education with the order of St Vladimir dangling round his neck. There is certainly nothing revolutionary or remarkable in that old-fashioned, slightly ridiculous figure, and yet Ilya Ulyanov could be proud of his achievements. In ascending the ladder of official promotions, he had reached the rank of full state counsellor, which brought with it elevation to the status of hereditary nobility and entitled him to be addressed as 'Your Excellency'. Lenin himself never omitted to enter this status in every record and never addressed his letters to his mother, to whom he was devoted, otherwise than as 'Her Excellency'.

In 1886 Lenin's father died suddenly at the age of fifty-five, leaving his large family with a modest pension supplemented by the private income of his widow, who inherited with her brothers and sisters a substantial estate in the Samara province called Kokushkino. This came from her father, a certain Alexander Blank, a physician who, according to Lenin's biographers, had

Left: A picture of respectability — the Ulyanov family in 1879. The family ties were close-knit and Lenin (on the right) was devoted to his mother. All the children became revolutionaries

retired to the estate near Samara and busied himself giving medical assistance to the local peasants. The lack of curiosity displayed by Soviet historians about Lenin's maternal grandfather is surprising. According to recent research made by distinguished Jewish scholars in the West, Blank began as a Jewish medical orderly in the Russian army, was converted to Greek Orthodoxy, studied, became a doctor, and settled in Samara. Did Lenin know about his grandfather? The status of a Jew who had become Orthodox was peculiar in the Russian conditions of that time. To the Jews, he was a damned apostate. To the Russians, he was suspect as having made a deal with his conscience. A Jewish ancestry was difficult to live down in spite of the fact that conversion meant total assimilation.

Lenin himself marks the year of the death of his father as that of his religious crisis. The Ulyanov household must have been typical of the homes of innumerable Russian officials living in distant provincial towns, with the boredom of daily routine only interrupted by the boredom of social intercourse, dinners, and card-playing. Religion, that is the observance of the liturgical cycle year by year with obligatory fasting followed by over-eating on feast-days, must have been the rule there as anywhere else in that stuffy atmosphere. Lenin gives no explanation for his crisis of faith. It may have been simply the shedding of a routine habit by an intelligent and self-opinionated youth, and as such would have passed entirely unnoticed.

The year after Ilya Ulyanov's death brought a much greater tragedy to the family. Alexander Ulyanov, Vladimir's elder by four years, who had been an outstanding student of natural science in St Petersburg University, became involved in revolutionary activities and took part in a plot to assassinate Tsar Alexander III. Arrested with a number of others, he displayed considerable courage and defiance during his trial, but was sentenced to death and executed on 8th May 1887. His mother was given to understand that an appeal for mercy to the Tsar by the delinquent might save his life. This he refused to do out of a spirit of defiance, and significantly his mother did not press him to comply with the authorities' paternalistic advice.

Alexander Naumov, who shared Lenin's desk at school for six years, writes: 'Vladimir Ulyanov was undoubtedly the central figure among our classmates. During all the six years of our time together at school, he was top of the

Far right: Lenin as a student, 1891 (top) and Alexander, the brother whom he admired and who was executed for plotting to kill the Tsar. Right: The younger Ulyanovs Maria and Dmitri

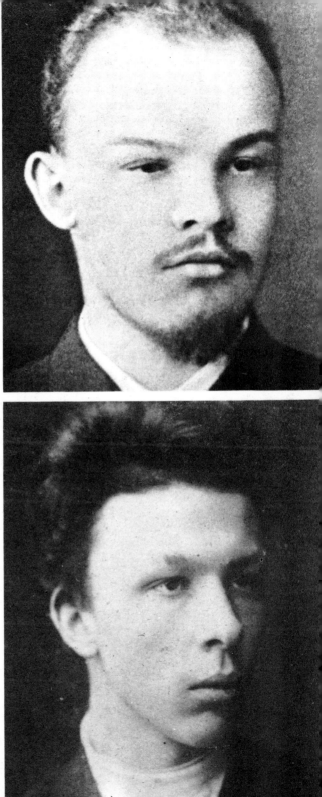

form and I was runner-up. Accordingly, on finishing the course he was awarded the gold and I the silver medal.

'Rather short, but fairly powerfully built, with slightly hunched-up shoulders and a large head, slightly compressed at the sides, Vladimir Ulyanov had irregular and, I would say, unhandsome features: small ears, prominent cheekbones, a short, wide, slightly squashed nose, and, in addition, a large mouth with yellow, widely-spaced teeth. With no eyebrows on his freckled face, Ulyanov had longish blond, soft and slightly curly hair which he combed straight back. But all these irregularities were redeemed by his high forehead, under which burned two fierce little brown eyes. His ungainly appearance was easily forgotten in conversation under the effect of these small but unusual eyes which sparkled with extraordinary intelligence and energy . . .

'At school Ulyanov differed considerably from all of us, his comrades. Neither in the lower forms nor later did he take part in the childish and youthful games and pranks, always keeping to himself, busy either with his studies or some written work. Even when walking between classes, Ulyanov kept to his books, reading as he walked up and down past the windows. The only thing which he liked as a distraction was playing chess, a game in which he usually came out victorious, even when playing against several opponents . . .'

According to Naumov, Vladimir Ulyanov was gifted, keen, possessed with insatiable, scholarly curiosity and extraordinary capacity for work. He was 'a walking encyclopaedia, extremely useful to his comrades and the pride of his teachers'.

'As soon as he appeared in the form Ulyanov was immediately surrounded by schoolmates who asked him for a translation or for the solution of a problem. He helped everybody willingly, but it seemed to me at that time that he nevertheless resented those who tried to live and do their schoolwork at the expense of another's labour and intellect.

'Ulyanov had an even and rather gay temperament, but he was extremely secretive and cool in his relations with comrades: he had no friends. He said "you" to everybody [instead of the "thou" common amongst schoolmates in Russia] and I do not remember a single time when he would unbend and allow himself to be intimately outspoken with me. On the whole, he commanded respect and displayed businesslike authority to his comrades, but one couldn't say that he was liked, rather that he was esteemed, and although everyone in the form realised his intellectual and scholarly superiority over all of us, it is only fair to point out that Ulyanov never flaunted it.'

Although this characterisation was written in the

twenties, it is particularly interesting as Naumov had every reason to feel political hatred for his former schoolmate. An ex-official and even Minister of the Crown in Russia, he wrote his memoirs in the emigration to which Lenin's October Revolution had forced him. The aloofness which Naumov points out and which is so typical of Lenin's later conspiratorial activities served him well on completing high school. Had he been more outspoken, about either his religious crisis or Alexander's execution, his headmaster, Fedor Kerensky (as though by contrivance of fate, the father of Lenin's chief adversary in 1917), could never have supported his application to the university. In this testimonial Kerensky assured the authorities that the young candidate had an excellent and pious education and that his mother would follow him to Kazan to see that he did not fall under bad influences.

The first revolutionary stirrings

In spite of all Fedor Kerensky's assurances, which were probably both benevolent and sincere, Lenin and also his sisters had already decided on their future position in Russian society. The last years of Alexander III's reign were marked by a sharp decline in the rapid and near-revolutionary development of the first half of his father Alexander II's reign. The institutions introduced in the sixties, the abolition of serfdom, the transfer of administrative authority in the Russian village from the landowner to the peasant community (mir), the reform of the judiciary with the introduction of 'open, oral, swift, and just' trials, the profound reform of the army with general conscription and a considerable reduction of state privileges, the educational reforms – all these innovations had produced side-effects which had frightened the paternalistic, bureaucratic, and idealistically dedicated government of Alexander III. Measures were introduced which distorted and destroyed the lofty purpose of the reforms of the sixties.

Nevertheless, the spirit of public service so prevalent in Russian educated society during the reform period survived in the succeeding reign. If we take the life history of Alexander Naumov, whose evaluation of Lenin's character we have quoted, we find that he decided to serve as an administrative officer for peasant affairs in exactly that part of Russia where Lenin was gradually building up his own character as a revolutionary. The two careers run parallel, but Naumov's approach to the Russian situation was empirical, tolerant, and reformist,

Left: Tsarist police make an arrest. Alexander Ulyanov, in contrast to Lenin, advocated terror to undermine the regime

whereas that of Lenin very soon became doctrinaire, abstract, intolerant, and rebellious. What was it that caused Lenin to join the revolutionary movement in Russia, which was still far from organised politically, not yet supported by academic and scholarly circles, devoid of a real knowledge of the conditions in which the people lived whom the revolutionary wanted to help, and full of contempt for their hopes and desires, which were set too low for the enthusiastic revolutionary?

We can safely dismiss any literary and theoretical influence on the formation of Lenin's revolutionary attitude at the age of sixteen. There is no truth in the report that he had been acquainted with the works of Marx in his schooldays. Nor should we attach too much importance to the story of Vladimir's conversion to a revolutionary creed by the influence of his elder brother, who, although critical of Vladimir's character, was an authority and an object of hero-worship to the younger brother. Alexander Ulyanov made at his trial a particularly noble attempt to relieve his fellow-conspirators of responsibility, claiming much of the incriminating activity onto his own account. One would expect him to have been even more careful not to involve any member of his family in his political activities, although he might have betrayed his extreme political views in the intimacy of his own family.

Yet it can hardly be doubted that Lenin was already intent on joining the revolutionary movement in Russia when he finished his secondary education, for he became a member of an underground circle of a fairly innocuous character as soon as he arrived in Kazan to start on his university course. We think the explanation of this sequence of events does not present any great psychological problem. The fact of his being the brother of a 'state criminal' who went to the gallows would necessarily reflect on Lenin's future career in Russia. But this alone would not mean that he would become an object of political persecution. There were no difficulties in his becoming a student in Kazan. Any career was open to him, and the Russian State and the Tsarist administration did not practise the persecution of relatives of state criminals as such. Lenin could easily have become a state official, a worker in local government, a lawyer, fully independent of state control, if not of state interference, or even a university professor, a career to which his extraordinary capacity for digesting abstruse reading material seemed to predestine him. Yet he apparently rejected all these possibilities by joining one of those circles which the police were closely watching at that

Left: Tsar Nicholas II, last of the Romanovs, and his mother

19

time and which sooner or later would have contributed to his being classified in the official records as a 'politically unreliable' person. Had he, however, chosen a 'respectable' career, he might still have felt that he had something to live down, something to explain at every step of promotion. From the description of his character given by Naumov, we may imagine how difficult psychologically this would have been for the young Ulyanov. On the other hand, within the revolutionary sub-culture or 'dissident establishment' in Russia at that time, the affair of Lenin's brother would be regarded not as a disadvantage but as a positive asset. Indeed, Vladimir encountered in student groups a keen interest and a desire to foster his progress as the young brother of so noble a victim and martyr.

The social formation in which Lenin could hope to find a place for his talents and energy is best described as a 'movement'. At that period it was more or less totally unorganised and profoundly split ideologically, its one uniting feature being the belief that only a radical change in the political and social structure of Russia could bring real progress to the people and that all attempts to secure development by gradual reform and elimination of the worst abuses were futile and even dangerous, because they disguised the perpetuation of an abominable regime and delayed the overthrow of the system embodied in the autocratic Tsarist bureaucracy. Different elements in the movement saw different ways of achieving this radical solution. Some believed in the awakening of political interest in the wide masses of the peasantry, who would claim political rights and control of state affairs through organisations already existing in Russia such as the peasant communes. Others combined these plans with the idea of permanent and relentless revolutionary terror, which, by decimating and demoralising the senior ranks of Tsarist bureaucracy, would bring about a capitulation of the supreme power and a transfer of its prerogatives to the representatives of the popular masses. Others again derided the romantic populist belief in the ability of the Russian peasantry to create a rational social order which alone could bring justice to the country and to humanity. It was among these last that a few writings of Marx, in Russian translation since the 1860s, found acceptance. They believed that every human society developed in sequential stages according to an immutable natural law: primitive subsistence economy, slave-state, feudal society, bourgeois revolution, capitalist expansion, and finally, as a crowning culmination, the great proletarian revolution leading humanity to its ultimate destination—Communist order. Inside this Marxist strain of the Russian revolutionary movement one could early on discern certain variations, but the main ideological debate of the time was centred on the quarrel between the Populists and the Marxists.

It appears that at the time when Lenin decided to be a revolutionary, or found that he was one, he had no idea which of these movements he was joining, nor had he any criterion for deciding which of them was right and which wrong. There was little opportunity for him to decide before his arrival in Kazan.

Lenin left Simbirsk for his university studies with his whole family; he was duly entered as a student and immediately joined a small illegal circle of students where questions of politics or revolutionary doctrine and practice were discussed. On 4th December 1887 a disturbance took place in Kazan University in which Lenin seems to have played no active part. However, his name was taken by the police and he was arrested that night. He must have been released the following day for we have a rather truculent letter from him to the Rector of Kazan University, in which he says: 'I do not consider it possible to carry on my education at the University under the present conditions of university life,' and he asks to be dismissed – a favour granted by the Rector without delay. He continued, however, to live in Kazan with the family until May 1888. At the beginning of that month he applied for readmission to the University, but as he had been put under the secret surveillance of the police after the December fracas, the university authorities refused to admit him.

For the next two years Lenin was constantly watched by the police, whether at Kokushkino, in Kazan, or on a small estate near the village of Alakaevka in the Samara province. These were years of intensive study, both of the subjects taught at the Russian Law Faculties and of the literature in which Lenin sought the theoretical foundation for his revolutionary attitude. He made several attempts to re-enter a university or at least to be admitted to the final examinations at a Faculty of Law. All his applications were rejected, including his request for a passport to leave Russia and complete his education abroad. When, in consideration of an application by his mother, he was at last allowed to take his final examinations in St Petersburg University, his performance was outstanding.

Left: A Russian socialist cartoon of 1900 depicts the oppression of the peasants and the working classes. 'We rule you' (Emperor), 'We guide you' (government), 'We fool you' (priests), 'We shoot you' (army), 'We eat off you' (bourgeoisie)

Chapter 2

The Revolutionary Movement

The brilliant end of his university studies would have given Lenin the opportunity to embark on a career which would help him to maintain his family. His first step was, however, to try to obtain a passport to go abroad immediately and only when this was refused did he return to Samara (now Kuybyshev) where he took up a job as assistant to a local lawyer. His frequent application to the authorities to be regraded as a fully-fledged solicitor should not mislead us into thinking that he took a normal career as family breadwinner at all seriously. On the contrary, Lenin was permanently occupied with reading Russian revolutionary literature of all kinds including Marxist. Wherever he lived he joined small circles which discussed revolutionary problems. These activities were the result—and not the cause—of his revolutionary attitude. By the summer of 1893 Lenin, ready for something more ambitious, naturally chose to move to the revolutionary centre of gravity—the capital.

His dead brother's reputation preceded him to St Petersburg, and he was thus assured of an invitation to join one of the revolutionary circles. For a year he divided his time between earning a living as a lawyer and engaging in the predominantly theoretical pursuits of the circle. His contact with workers did not come at once. Indeed Russian Marxists at that time had not yet discovered an effective means of achieving such contacts. Then in 1894 he gave up his job and devoted himself wholly to publicising his views in Marxist journals (permitted by the censorship) and to acquiring a reputation as one of the most forceful debaters in that milieu.

St Petersburg in the 1890s was the bustling centre of the Russian revolutionary sub-culture. Large numbers of intellectuals of all shades of revolutionary opinion thronged its clandestine meeting-places. Outstanding as both a theoretician and a man of numerous contacts, as well as provider of funds for Marxist publications, was Peter Struve. Struve was prominent in a group of socio-

Left: Lenin (centre), known as the 'old man', and Martov (seated right), his friend and later rival, in the Petersburg Union of Struggle for the Liberation of the Working Class, 1897

МОСКОВСКОЕ ОХРАННОЕ ОТДѢЛЕНІЕ.

logically oriented intellectuals known as 'legal Marxists', who were less concerned with Marx's revolutionary message than with his system of analysis and interpretation of the processes of social development, for their primary purpose was at that time to determine exactly what was happening to Russia under the impact of the government's policy of intensive industrialisation. They were engaged in fierce and endless polemics with the Populists, who argued that capitalism was still relatively primitive in Russia.

The Populists hoped that Russia might be able to reach socialism without having to pass through a capitalist phase, thanks to the existence of collectivist and indeed socialist traditions in the agricultural activity· of Russian peasantry. This approach, which repudiated the Marxist pattern of social development for Russia, based as it was on industrialisation, appealed strongly both to the peasantry and to many intellectuals, and gave rise to the formation in 1902 of a Socialist Revolutionary party, known by its initials of SR. (The SRs absorbed the tradition of political terrorism from the Russian past and were to play a short but important part during the turbulent years of 1905 and 1917.) It was the efficacy of the 'legal Marxists'' attacks on the Populists that attracted Lenin to the idea proposed personally by Struve that they collaborate in a new journal designed to spread the doctrine to an even wider public of both the intelligentsia and the workers. While taking these steps to form an intellectual alliance with Struve, Lenin was writing articles and reviews in which he vehemently took Struve to task for his optimistic view of the progressive role of the bourgeoisie.

In the spring of 1895 Lenin was chosen to visit the émigré leaders of the Russian Marxist movement in Switzerland. George Plekhanov and Paul Axelrod were both veterans of the Populist movement of the 1870s and had emigrated to Switzerland, along with hundreds of others, at the end of that decade to evade the police. By 1883 they—especially Plekhanov—had established themselves as the ideological leaders of the nascent Marxist revolutionary movement in Russia. Though they were of widely different social background—Plekhanov an ex-officer cadet and Axelrod the son of a poor Jewish innkeeper—they nonetheless maintained their friendship and collaboration for decades, splitting up, like so many other friends, only upon the great issue of Russian policy in the First World War. Lenin came to them in order to

Left: The police picture of Lenin taken on the day of his arrest in 1895 (top) and the peasant's house in Shushenskoe, Siberia, where Lenin spent three years in contented exile (bottom)

25

secure their support for the new publishing venture. This was to be his first visit abroad. Plekhanov was in principle in favour of the proposed co-operation, but evidently found in Lenin's attacks on the 'legal Marxists' some underlying inconsistency in his disciple's attitude: 'You show the liberals your backside. It is our policy to confront them face to face.' The fundamental incompatibility in social democratic revolutionary and liberal evolutionary aims was something fully recognised by Plekhanov and Axelrod, but they also saw that Russian revolutionary Marxism lacked both organisation and means and must accept collaboration with the liberal democrats in a less doctrinaire spirit.

Probably content to dismiss the young revolutionary's doctrinal slips as the result of political euphoria, Plekhanov and Axelrod alike felt that he was the man best suited to carry through the difficult practical side of the venture. The smuggling into Russia and distribution there of illegal revolutionary literature, and still more the regular handling of a newspaper under the sharp eye of the security police, were tasks fraught with danger of arrest and deportation. However, if the Marxist social democratic movement was to develop momentum it must achieve much wider adherence among the workers themselves and no less must it contribute its own identifiable fire to the battle of words being waged against the Populists.

Lenin's return to St Petersburg later that year coincided with the arrival from Vilna of Julius Martov. Martov, whose real name was Tsederbaum, was raised in the tradition of the enlightened and recently russified Jewish intelligentsia, a man of sensitive yet strangely dogmatic disposition. Martov had spent two years combining his experience as a young revolutionary with a kind of trade union activity which flourished among the Jewish artisans living in the Pale of Settlement, that is, those provinces in the south and west of the Russian Empire to which Jews, with few exceptions, were restricted. Instead of joining small self-improvement circles, which only isolated them from their class, the workers were encouraged by the social democrats to strike systematically for economic gains which would, it was assumed, bring them eventually into conflict with the state which protected the capitalist system. In this process the workers would gradually learn political awareness and be prepared for their role in the socialist revolution.

Martov brought this system of ideas and methods with him to St Petersburg where they were received enthusiastically by jaded intellectuals, bewildered by their lack of success among the workers. Lenin was also

enthusiastic and he and Martov took well to each other. Indeed theirs was one of the rare friendships of Lenin's life which sparked sufficient intimacy for this difficult man to address Martov in the familiar 'thou'.

But Martov's 'method' had its hazards; in particular it brought its practitioners into close contact with the workers and thus exposed them as easy prey to the ever-watchful security police. No later than December 1895, ten members of that revolutionary group including Martov and Lenin were arrested. After a spell in St Petersburg prison both men were banished to Siberia by administrative order for a period of three years.

Lenin in Siberia

The years Lenin spent in banishment in Siberia were very possibly the happiest of his life. He had with him the manuscript of a large work he had been writing while in prison in St Petersburg, a Marxist interpretation of the economic situation in Russia. Books were made available to him by his relatives and friends. The girl he intended to marry joined him soon after his arrival in Shushenskoe in Eastern Siberia. He enjoyed the dry, continental climate of Siberia and would go for long walks or sleigh-rides carrying his sports gun with him. Financially his situation was also quite satisfactory. Besides the pittance which the Tsarist government paid to people living on their own in banishment, he received quite substantial sums of money from his mother. He also undertook, with the help of his future wife, Nadezhda Krupskaya, to translate *The Theory and Practice of Trade Unionism* by Sidney and Beatrice Webb. He maintained a lively correspondence with political friends in European Russia and Switzerland, and with fellow exiles in Siberia. All these activities helped establish him as a theoretical and practical revolutionary in the small but influential circles of irreconcilable rebels against the existing regime, which had by then sprung up in many widely scattered places in the Russian Empire. This does not mean that Lenin was anything of a public figure. Extreme political dissidents were cut off from every stratum of Russian society except the oppositionist intelligentsia. Lenin as a politician was therefore hardly noticeable and it would be surprising if one in a hundred thousand of the population had ever heard his name, whether it be Ulyanov

*Left: The early revolutionaries. **Left-hand column from top:** Krupskaya, whose marriage with Lenin was to last for life; Plekhanov and Axelrod, émigré founders of Russian Marxism; Maxim Gorky, world-famous writer and fund-raiser for Lenin.* ***Right-hand column:*** *Inessa Armand, who became a Bolshevik in 1904 and later Lenin's close friend; Trotsky, 'the young eagle'; Stalin; Lunacharsky, later Soviet Commissar for Education*

or one of the pen-names under which he invariably published his work. His major socio-economic study, *The Development of Capitalism in Russia*, was signed V. Ilyin and only his personal friends and correspondents knew it to be his.

This book remains Lenin's major contribution to Russian economic thought. It also bears the typical imprint of his approach to any theoretical subject which had a bearing, direct or indirect, on his political aspirations. His analysis of official statistics was laced with violent and scurrilous attacks on fellow-researchers in the same field. He was especially vitriolic against those who believed that Russia's path to socialism lay along a route different from that predicted by Marx for industrialised societies. According to Lenin, in spite of economic and technical backwardness Russia had already reached that stage of social differentiation in which the conflict of classes was clearly distinguishable. Therefore a situation existed which revolutionaries should exploit in order to carry the conflict through to their ultimate goal and its culmination – the socialist revolution led by the industrial proletariat. Incidentally, Lenin's stratification of the rural population (that is, over eighty-five per cent of the total population) into the poor, medium, and rich, as a recipe for inevitable class conflict even among peasants, remained an axiom of Leninism up to his last reform when he was already in power – the introduction in 1922 of the New Economic Policy.

Lenin encountered no resistance from the Tsarist censor when it came to having his book published. It was far too academic to be regarded as a political tract, and besides, the censorship, less single-minded than the secret police, had not yet fully realised the subversive potential of Marxist economic theory. By the time Lenin completed his allotted three years in Siberia, his book was already out and he could return to European Russia an established specialist in economics, and in particular in Marxist economics.

In 1894 he had met in St Petersburg Nadezhda Krupskaya, a fellow-revolutionary, ex-schoolmistress, and daughter of an unsuccessful army officer. She was exiled on her own account shortly after Lenin, and she joined him in Siberia, where they were married, in church, in 1898. When Lenin departed at the end of his term of exile, Krupskaya remained behind for almost another year to complete her own term. The couple remained devoted to each other throughout their lives. Krupskaya accepted without murmur all the privations which the life of political emigration chosen by both of them imposed. She kept a close watch on Lenin's health and guarded him from intruders who wasted his time in fruitless theoretical

discussions. More than that, she conducted all his correspondence, operated the secret codes, and mastered other methods of clandestine communication, primitive though they were. It seems that as time went on, common political interests replaced the more personal elements in their relationship, though when Krupskaya fell ill with a serious thyroid disease, Lenin took great trouble to get her better, and insisted in 1913 on an operation in a Swiss clinic.

Lenin accepted the permanent presence of his mother-in-law of whom he was very fond and who is reputed to be the one person in his entourage who would stand no nonsense from him. Even so, there is no doubt that Krupskaya was not the only woman in Lenin's emotional life; his later contacts with Inessa Armand, a Russo-French revolutionary of whom, it seems, Lenin became very fond, were also of considerable political importance.

Strife among the Marxists

During Lenin's exile the Russian Marxist revolutionary movement underwent substantial change, not least as a result of intense and effective police persecution. The Marxist intellectuals found that their efforts to build a bridge to the working masses by means of small workers' circles had the countereffect of creating instead a working-class elite which became increasingly detached from its class origins and interests. On the other hand the movement based on mass agitation which replaced the circles of the mid-1890s was frustrated from the workers' point of view by police interference.

This apparent total incompatibility between workers and intellectuals received a measure of ideological support at the turn of the century from the revision of certain basic tenets of Marxism by Eduard Bernstein, the German Social Democrat. Questioning the concept of class struggle, Bernstein explicitly advocated separation of the labour movement from political struggle, since the middle class could be trusted to fight for democratic liberties on behalf of society as a whole.

This new formulation resulted in a major split among Marxists. According to one school of thought, represented overwhelmingly by semi-academic journalists, economists, and philosophers, the Russian Marxists need no longer toil at the slow and futile task of educating, propagandising, or organising the workers in their economic struggle. Instead they could free themselves to concentrate on purely political work together with the

Top left: Lenin's unofficial record of the Second Congress, held in London in 1903. Bottom: The first issue of Iskra, printed on onion-skin paper in Germany and smuggled into Russia

29

radical leaders of the liberal movement. As for the workers, let them continue to concern themselves with their economic worries: their political future would be secured for them when democracy was won.

A very different, strongly negative, reaction to Bernstein's revisions of Marx and still more powerfully to the Russians who swallowed them was voiced by Marxists who would henceforth be known as the revolutionary wing of Russian social democracy, as opposed to its evolutionary wing. Of these the most passionate and eventually most potent critic of the new trend was Lenin. Ringingly he denounced as typical middle-class intellectuals – what worse insult was ever to be found in Lenin's canon of invective? – these Revisionists, with their despicable betrayal of the masses to the swindle of 'economism'. If the workers were not ready for their allotted historical role, this was no cause for abandoning revolution in favour of evolution. No, another means must be found to make the revolution, but on no account in alliance with the congenitally treacherous bourgeoisie. As Plekhanov had remarked to him in 1895, Lenin showed his backside to the middle classes.

Gradually but clearly formulating his ideas on revolution and organisation, Lenin finally crystallised a system in 1902 in his famous treatise *What is to be done?* He believed, and profoundly so, that autonomous working-class action could never transcend the barrier of 'trade-union' consciousness, that the workers were not capable by themselves of thinking politically, that their world-view was circumscribed by the categories of capitalist relationships. Their enormous revolutionary potential, however, he did not underrate and envisaged harnessing it to the developed conscious drive of his own party. His party was to consist of a small, highly compact, disciplined band of professional revolutionaries acting in the name of the Russian workers but maintaining maximum security against the inroads either of the police or of the initiative of the workers. 'Give us a handful of revolutionaries and we will overturn Russia.' The medium through which Lenin was to express these ideas was his newspaper *Iskra* (The Spark), which would be transported clandestinely into Russia by a network of agents who would themselves embody the authority of Lenin's organisation. He established this arrangement in collaboration with his friend Julius Martov, and the first issue of *Iskra* appeared in December 1900.

Birth of the Bolsheviks
From 1900, living in Western Europe, Lenin began to prepare for a major Congress of the Russian Social Democratic Workers' Party at which the *Iskra* organisation

was planned to emerge as the controlling centre. The party itself had been organised in 1898 at its First Congress which took place in Russia. The police, however, destroyed virtually all its apparatus within weeks, leaving an empty shell in which Lenin planned to create the new party.

But at the Second Congress, held in London in the summer of 1903, a clash took place. In private meetings of the inner *Iskra* circle at the Congress it quickly became clear that Lenin was out to gain complete control of all the party institutions, and even though his scheme included Martov at its centre, Martov was affronted, as were many others, by the outright machiavellian nature of Lenin's tactics. The issue upon which Martov and Lenin openly revealed their divergence was the first clause of the party statutes dealing with membership. Each submitted his own draft. For Lenin, a member was one who accepted the programme and actively supported the party by taking part in one of the party organisations. Martov defined a member as one who accepted the programme, gave material support to the party and regular personal support under the guidance of one of its organisations. The difference between the two drafts need never have been elevated to the level of essential philosophical discord that in fact resulted, had there not already existed deep suspicion on Martov's part and anxious impatience for the safety of his plans on Lenin's part. But the heated discussions revealed that Martov's formula allowed for a wider and more loosely associated type of membership, while Lenin was implementing his plan for a party of professional revolutionaries. Lenin called for total control of the party from the centre; Martov urged the party to allow for differences of opinion among the rank and file.

The Congress split into two wings of almost equal magnitude. However, taking advantage of a momentary and marginal swing in the voting, Lenin named his supporters Bolsheviks, that is, belonging to the majority, while Martov's supporters became known as the Mensheviks, or those belonging to the minority. In political terms, the Bolsheviks prided themselves as 'rock-hard' revolutionaries, whereas the Mensheviks believed themselves to be the representatives of true Social Democracy. Lenin called them 'softs', for allowing their tolerant disposition to interfere with their political judgment; they would wait slavishly for 'History' to set the stage for revolution. Lenin saw things differently: if 'History' took too long getting there, then the revolutionaries must give 'History' a shove.

Left: Unrest spreads. A strike of Russian railway workers, 1905

After 1903 Lenin's impatience with the opinions of others and the vehemence of his expression led him into a succession of quarrels, temporary agreements, and violent breaks with close collaborators. He was determined to lead the party and no means were to be rejected which could achieve his end. The Bolsheviks were earning a reputation not only for zeal but for adventurism.

The false dawn of 1905

The revolution of 1905 brought Lenin back to Russia with high hopes that an armed insurrection could be organised to overthrow Tsarism. A workers' council (soviet) had been formed in St Petersburg which earned from Lenin no more than tentative approval while he was still in Europe: he was not one to subscribe to amateurish notions of workers' government. The leader of the St Petersburg Soviet was a dynamic young revolutionary called Trotsky, whom Lenin had once cherished as a disciple and who was now magnetising the crowds with revolutionary oratory. Lenin decided not to compete on that particular stage, but instead vanished into a twilight world, preparing for an armed insurrection in which the main part would, so he hoped, be his. But the Tsar's October 1905 Manifesto promising, however grudgingly, an elected assembly effectively reduced the enormous public pressure for change, and the army had little difficulty in dealing with all armed revolutionary groups. In January 1907, the revolution extinguished, Lenin again left Russia, not to return for another ten years.

This second exile was especially depressing for the revolutionaries: the state had shown an astonishing resistance to revolutionary onslaught even though weakened by a disastrous defeat in the war with Japan. Lenin's grandiose plan for an organisation of professional revolutionaries had foundered, and in time every Russian Social Democrat with a mind of his own abandoned him in favour of a more independent life. Every shade of opinion expressed by anyone but Lenin himself he converted to fuel for the factional fire. The Mensheviks often made matters worse by playing the same game, and many Social Democrats, notably Trotsky, ran foul of both sides by trying to bridge the two. It particularly irritated Lenin that a number of Bolshevik intellectuals, whose literary support he badly needed, had found a rival leader in the brilliant philosopher-revolutionary Bogdanov, who combined erudition with great organisational skill.

Events in Russia after 1907 only sharpened Lenin's sense of futility. What if the government's reforms

Left: Lenin plays chess in Capri with the leading philosopher-Bolshevik Bogdanov (on right), while Gorky (above) looks on

33

should succeed and Russia could at last settle down to a steady development of her capitalist economy? The Russian monarchy had survived; the war with Japan, though a disgrace to Russia, had ended with a lenient peace settlement; foreign loans underwrote the economy; the rebellious people had been silenced, and the vociferous middle class had been given a safe place in the State Duma, in which they could ventilate their ideas to their hearts' content, albeit with small general effect. What were revolutionaries to do now? One answer was provided by the intelligentsia at large, both in Russia and abroad. In Russia the mood which arose in the aftermath of 1905 was one of seeking for a system of ethics of a less political character than that which had so absorbed previous generations of intellectuals.

The revolution had come and gone, certain changes had taken place, one could vote for one's choice of Duma deputy, one could read a wider range of less severely censored newspapers, one could note with gratification that the workers were being gradually allowed to have their unions. Above all it was clear the government was doing something positive about the land-hunger of the great mass of peasantry. Prime Minister Stolypin's reforms were directed at the creation of a large sector of stable and industrious independent smallholders, and even if his purpose was to establish a rural ballast against future unrest, the effect on peasant life itself must surely turn out to be beneficial.

This possibility was not lost on Lenin and altogether these developments were sourly viewed by him as the portents of a prolonged phase of political apathy in Russia. And he was right in this assumption. A mood of contemplation overtook Russia's small but highly articulate minority of intellectuals. Speculative philosophy and human psychology, aesthetics and morals almost totally displaced materialistic political economics in the minds of the revolutionary and liberal intelligentsia. When some Bolshevik intellectuals, like the philosopher Bogdanov, the future Soviet Commissar for Education Lunacharsky, and the great Russian writer Maxim Gorky, joined in the search for a metaphysical interpretation of the revolution and claimed that it was for the spiritual emancipation and exaltation of man, and not for a redistribution of wealth under the dictatorship of the proletariat, it was too much for Lenin to stand. Bogdanov, who had been one of Lenin's closest collaborators since 1904, was one of the members of the tiny, secret Bolshevik Centre, a group within the central

Left: 'The Blind Tsar' – German left-wing comment on the brutal massacre of unarmed workers on 'Bloody Sunday', January 1905

body of the party, and his intellectual powers and independent stand on a number of subjects made him an especially sharp thorn in Lenin's side, now that once again all attention must needs be focused on inner party relationships instead of directed outwards to social action. When control of party funds became a bone of contention between Lenin and Bogdanov, Lenin decided it was time to act.

His attack on all this 'intellectual necrophilia' was blistering, and it brought about his isolation from the one remaining group of Bolshevik writers and intellectuals with whom he had been involved. From 1907 until the First World War Lenin lost the support and friendship one by one of virtually the entire Bolshevik intelligentsia. Since it was he who invariably drew the line marking off loyalty and orthodoxy from outright betrayal, or at best backsliding, he could never join anyone but must hold his fort alone until reinforcements arrived of their own free will.

In spite of the languor which had overtaken the Russian intelligentsia since its militant phase had died down, much was going on in Russia and political parties did take up positions on practical issues. The most important decision for the Russian Social Democrats concerned participation in the Duma. At first all groups and wings of the party were against taking part in the pseudo-parliamentary farce, which was roughly their understanding of this institution. But when, in the First Duma, which sat in 1906, it appeared that the liberals, with their overwhelming majority, had found a wonderful public platform for making their progressive propaganda, many Social Democrats changed their minds. In the Second Duma Bolsheviks and Mensheviks gained about one seventh of all the seats which, though few, nonetheless gave them a voice alongside all the other revolutionary parties. It was indeed the manifest opportunity for propaganda which the Duma provided that prompted Stolypin to change the electoral laws so as to weight the assembly towards the right-wing moderate, compliant if not pro-government parties, turning the Third Duma into virtually a rubber-stamp for his own projects.

Lenin had been quick to advocate participation on the same ground as the Mensheviks, that of exploitation of the institution as a sounding board. But the Bolsheviks around Bogdanov, calling themselves the 'Forward' group, had opposed participation on the grounds that any compromise must emasculate Bolshevik policy, and demanded the recall of the party's deputies.

Left: The blood-stained rainbow over Moscow in 1905 failed to herald the uprising that Lenin hoped would stir the masses

Throughout the period following the split in 1903 right up to 1917 there is a clearly discernible trend among the Russian Social Democrats to make common cause and repair the breach between the two factions. Lenin is the outstanding exception. In an attempt to give his position the force of legality, Lenin organised a conference, in January 1912 in Prague, at which a tiny number of totally unrepresentative delegates, unrepresentative even on their own recognition, allowed Lenin to declare their meeting the Sixth All-Russian Conference of the Party, and thus to proclaim the separate identity of the Bolsheviks as a party. But past elections had shown that the workers wanted to have Social Democratic deputies, and although in the Fourth Duma the Bolsheviks only managed to get in six of their men and the Mensheviks only seven, the two factions found themselves so nearly in accord in their parliamentary roles that in 1912 they tried to bury the factional hatchet and work together. The editors of the Bolshevik newspaper *Pravda*, Stalin and Molotov, made subtle cuts in Lenin's articles in order to damp down their anti-Menshevik heat. Lenin was enraged by these developments and set about splitting up the factions again.

In this aim he was aided by the Tsarist security police. They planted Roman Malinovsky as an *agent provocateur* within Lenin's grasp. Malinovsky was an experienced workers' leader with the gift of fiery rhetoric. After one meeting Lenin approved him as a candidate to the Duma for the Bolsheviks. The police did their part by suppressing a criminal record in Malinovsky's past and by smoothing his electoral path. In 1912 he entered the Duma as the spokesman of the Bolshevik faction.

'In order to be closer to the Russian frontier' and thus to maintain easier contact with his 'wonderful workers' leader', Lenin moved to the Polish village of Poronino, near Cracow, in the Austro-Hungarian Empire. Malinovsky was a frequent visitor and quickly assumed an integral role in the transmission of Lenin's ideas to the Russian people by way of the Duma. He even spiced Lenin's already peppery speeches, designed to frighten off the Mensheviks. In his strategic position he effected a number of arrests by informing on Bolsheviks like Stalin who had been conducting a conciliatory policy. In 1913 Malinovsky's work was doubled in *Pravda* by another agent, Chernomazov, and by the end of the year they had succeeded in splitting the two Social Democratic factions of the Duma into two opposing groups once again. Malinovsky, who had already aroused intense suspicion among many Social Democrats, was in May 1914 relieved of his post by the Ministry of the Interior and gave up his seat in the Duma. But he did not go into

hiding on the Riviera, as he could so easily have done. Instead he ran to Lenin in Poronino to beg for the protection of a testimonial. Lenin's protestations in Malinovsky's defence were passionate, but in private he admitted that he was very worried by the whole business.

The Malinovsky affair was only one more nail that was being hammered into Lenin's coffin as a leader of the Russian socialist movement. He had been heavily compromised in 1907 by endorsing, and indeed by profiting from, a number of so-called 'expropriations', that is robberies, carried out both by *bona fide* bandits and by members of Lenin's faction. When arrests in Western Europe and the USA were made of some individuals bearing identified banknotes from one of these robberies, Bolshevik complicity was established and socialist indignation, both Russian and foreign, waxed against Lenin.

His intransigent fractiousness, which divided and weakened the movement, and his methods in trying to outflank the Mensheviks had earned him such a bad reputation in the Socialist International that this body decided to intervene by summoning him to a tribunal in Brussels, at which he was to answer the charges against him. Indignantly he refused to go, but sent instead his intimate friend Inessa Armand, with firm instructions to represent the Bolsheviks as a separate independent party taking orders from nobody. In the event the International Bureau passed an innocuous resolution calling on all groups to find common ground in the party programme. The Russians were enjoined to hold a general party congress at which the majority view must prevail for all. It was an empty wish for two reasons: first, because Lenin had already begun to organise his own 'Party Congress', where the Bolsheviks would once and for all finish with any attempt at unity; and secondly, because before either gathering could take place a completely new set of conditions was imposed on Europe, and most assuredly on the socialists within it, by the outbreak in July 1914 of the First World War.

Left: Crowds gather to hear the announcement of the Tsar's manifesto, October 1905. Trotsky wrote: 'Absolutism remains'

39

Chapter 3

Lenin in the First World War

The outbreak of the First World War must have surprised Lenin no less than many better-informed politicians of the time. True, in a letter to Maxim Gorky in 1913, when Russo-Austrian relations were under strain, Lenin expressed his hope that the diplomatic conflict would lead to a localised war, but at the same time he remarked jokingly that Franz Joseph and Nicholas II 'would not oblige'. His quip is important because it shows that Lenin viewed war as the fertile soil for revolution. It also shows indirectly that Lenin still believed in the solidarity of the world proletariat in the face of war. When things came to a head in the summer of 1914, the attitude of the Social Democrats and various other Labour parties was profoundly disappointing to Lenin. Those who supported the bourgeois governments of their countries in this time of national danger were considered open traitors to the cause of the working class in general and were never to be recognised again as comrades.

The war began dramatically for Lenin. He had been living in the small Polish village of Poronino close to the Russo-Austrian border, where his activities had not gone unnoticed by the local police. His mail in both directions was voluminous. He was visited by a stream of characters of a type hardly likely to inspire the confidence of police agents. It is not surprising, therefore, that as soon as general mobilisation was proclaimed Lenin and Zinoviev, who was staying with him, were put into the local prison. No doubt the Austrian police were exercising a general precaution against citizens of an enemy state and the stories of danger to the lives of Lenin and Zinoviev are much exaggerated. Far more important than their arrest was the letter by which Lenin was freed and given permission to go to Switzerland. The Minister of the Interior, referring to the intervention of the Austrian Social Democrat, Victor Adler, wrote that, according to Dr Adler, 'Ulyanov could be of great use to us in the present situation'. Lenin was set free (together with Zinoviev) on

Left: Nicholas II, 'Autocrat of all the Russias', blesses the troops with an icon. But the strain of war was to erode their loyalty

19th August and went immediately to Vienna to arrange his journey to Switzerland. He was certainly moved by the realisation that he could maintain his political freedom only in a neutral country. Nevertheless, Victor Adler's assurance that he could be of use to the Central Powers was of immense importance for the entire pattern of Lenin's future activity.

The situation which he found among the émigrés in Switzerland filled him with anger and horror. Plekhanov, to whom the Russian socialists looked for leadership, proclaimed himself a determined supporter of the Entente powers. For him, a German victory would mean a return to nineteenth-century methods of administration and control in Russia as being the best means of German imperialist exploitation. On the other hand, a victory for the democratic bourgeois states would inevitably strengthen the democratic movement in Russia towards which Plekhanov had always looked for an alliance against Tsarist absolutism. Plekhanov went so far as to appeal to the Russian émigrés in France to join the French army, and many did. Without going so far as Plekhanov other socialists in France, including Martov, were still hoping for a concerted movement of the workers in the belligerent countries to put an end to the senseless slaughter and to press their governments to make peace, without annexations and indemnities. To these defencist and pacifist programmes Lenin opposed his own violent and undiluted defeatist propaganda. A few days after his arrival in Switzerland he delivered a speech at a public meeting in which he said: 'Chauvinism seeks to conceal itself in Russia behind such phrases as "la belle France", "the unfortunate Belgium", and behind hostility towards the Kaiser and his regime. Therefore it is our immediate duty to fight against this sophistry and for that we need a slogan to embrace the whole problem. Such a slogan should declare in a convincing way that from the point of view of the Russian working class defeat would be the lesser evil because Tsarism is a hundred times worse than the Kaiser's realm. "Peace" is not the right slogan at the present moment: it is the slogan of Christian priests and the lower middle classes. The proletarian slogan should be "Civil war"! While not in the position to promise a civil war or bring it about, it is our duty, if necessary for a long time to come, to persevere in this direction.'

The notion of transforming the war between nations

Top left: 'Everything for the war.' A Russian poster appeals for money. *Top right:* Russian field hospital. **Bottom:** The five Bolshevik deputies to the Fourth Duma in banishment in Siberia. They were convicted of high treason for encouraging defeatism

43

into a war between classes became the frame upon which Lenin spun the whole of his wartime propaganda. He had limited success among the Russian émigrés in Switzerland. In spite of occasional attacks on the Kaiser and the German government, Lenin's attitude was beyond doubt pro-German. When one of his closest followers expressed the fear that in case of defeat liberty and democracy would be lost for France, Lenin retorted: 'Let them be lost. France is nothing but a backward republic of usurers and rentiers who get fat on their gold. Should Germany, which is ahead of France industrially, conquer France there would be no harm in it. For us revolutionists this is completely irrelevant. Our task is to transform the imperialist war everywhere into a civil war.'

This was easier said than done. Plekhanov's influence among the émigrés asserted itself with his every public utterance. Moreover, never had Lenin felt so isolated from events in Russia. Direct communication with Russia was extremely difficult, and anyway the situation there seemed to reflect the confusion of ideas and behaviour prevailing throughout the rest of Europe.

The very air the proletarians in Russia breathed was polluted by chauvinism and imperialist propaganda. The party organisation seemed to be totally crushed. At the beginning of November 1914 a group of faithful Bolsheviks, including the Bolshevik members of the Duma, assembled in a small village near the Finnish border to discuss the practical implications of Lenin's defeatist doctrine. One of the innumerable secret agents betrayed the time and place of the meeting to the security police and all the participants were arrested and sent into banishment in remote regions of Siberia.

They took with them for the benefit of other exiles copies of Lenin's paper *Social-Democrat,* explaining Lenin's attitude to the war. It was accepted even by such future adversaries of Lenin as the Menshevik Tseretelli. The five Duma deputies who were seized along with the rest were also sentenced for spreading defeatist propaganda. Thus the Bolsheviks lost their representatives in the Duma at just the moment when a bloc opposed to the Tsarist government was about to come into being with the purpose of confronting that government with demands for radical constitutional change.

On the passive side of Lenin's policy during the war before 1917 the defection of some of his most ardent former followers was important. The fairly well-to-do Pyatakov and Rozmirovich claimed the unheard-of privilege of publishing their own Bolshevik journal at their own expense, offering Lenin no more than the

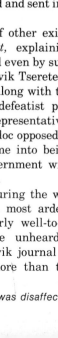

Right: *The Russian Baltic Fleet. The navy too was disaffected*

right to contribute. For Lenin, this development occurred at a most inopportune moment. There was no money in the party kitty and he had already spent most of what he had inherited from an aunt at the beginning of the war. Some of his Swiss wellwishers tried to explain to the Germans that the support of Lenin's propaganda might be of use to them. The Germans, however, through their main Russian agent, Dr Alexander Helphand-Parvus, had already tried to bring about a large-scale demonstration in Petrograd in January/February 1916. Although 100,000 people took part, including soldiers and workers, the attempt at revolution failed and the German government began to despair of achieving this aim during the war. This made them more stingy, and permission to subsidise the third issue of the magazine *Vestnik Sotsial-Demokrata* (Social Democratic Messenger), published by Lenin, was given only at the beginning of 1917 when the situation was, in any case, about to change radically.

The Germans also published their own newspapers in Russian intended mainly for Russian internees and prisoners-of-war. They would not, of course, try to involve Lenin in such publications. By 1915 they had been thoroughly informed by their agents, the Russian Parvus and the Estonian Keskuela, of Lenin's potential importance in case of sudden developments in the revolutionary situation in Russia and they would not want him to be compromised by his taking part in overt sedition. But people in his entourage such as Lilina, the wife of Zinoviev, had no scruples about printing propaganda in the German-sponsored press. In 1915, however, Lenin had had a lengthy meeting with Parvus, who came to Switzerland with the full knowledge and assistance of the German government in order to recruit Russian intellectuals for his so-called Scientific Institute in Copenhagen for the Study of the Social and Economic Consequences of the War. The meeting was inconclusive and Lenin refused to have anything to do with aims other than the fall of the Tsarist regime and the formation of a proletarian dictatorship under the guidance of the minuscule party over which he at that time presided. Parvus went back to Scandinavia where, powerfully supported by German secret funds, he continued his efforts to transform the ever-increasing wave of strikes in Russia into a major anti-government demonstration, which, as we have just seen, reached considerable dimensions in 1916. Lenin, however, went on with his pathetic attempts to undermine the morale of the munitions workers. His agents in Russia, few as they were, were always on the run and could do nothing beyond arguing against the defencist socialists and the patriotic feelings of the workers.

Deprived of the means to influence the course of

political development inside Russia, Lenin became increasingly embittered and intolerant. One of the victims of this mood was Bukharin, intellectually the most sophisticated of Lenin's entourage. The issue over which the two men now fell out was the national question. Bukharin advanced the strongly internationalist line that it was utopian to start agitating for the self-determination of all nations as long as capitalism still held sway. Moreover, the Bolshevik slogan of civil war implied the united efforts of internationally-minded working classes against all the forces of capitalism embodied in the militarist, industrial, and imperialist interests at play. For Bukharin and those grouped around him, the slogan of self-determination was also retrograde since it threatened to divide up the vast anti-capitalist potential of the proletariat at present being marshalled by the international conflict.

Lenin's propaganda during the war in favour of the demand by the nations of the Russian Empire for self-determination appeared to Bukharin as gross opportunism, nakedly aimed at the political dismemberment of the Russian state. This policy, however, fitted perfectly into the two-pronged programme being operated through Parvus by the Germans: to disrupt war production, and to break up the Empire by exacerbating and supporting national feeling among the borderland peoples. The polemics against Bukharin quickly assumed the customary Leninist tone of personal attack and denunciation. Bukharin, who preferred to keep such methods out of his political battles, appealed to Lenin not to allow the polemics to destroy their personal relationship, and in fact Lenin acquiesced and was about to publish Bukharin's views in his own journal when their debate was overwhelmed by the February Revolution of 1917.

During the time Lenin was without the support of this gifted and relatively honest follower he gained a valuable ally in the person of Alexandra Kollontay, who much later achieved a certain place in world history as the first ever woman ambassador and as an ardent advocate of free love. The daughter of a Russian general, she joined the revolutionary movement as a young, attractive woman, wrote some unreadable novels embodying her sexual philosophy, lived in Germany where she joined the German Social Democrats, and until the middle of the war regarded herself as a Menshevik. In 1914 she was expelled from Germany to Stockholm, whence she was again expelled in April 1916 together with Bukharin for their participation in a peace congress

Left: Fifteen million men were conscripted into the Tsar's armies; as many as 1,700,000 were killed on the battlefields

47

of Swedish workers. Having established herself in Oslo she undertook two voyages to the United States where she gave anti-war lectures to German communities and corresponded with Lenin, to whom she was now firmly pledged. Indeed, whatever her intellectual or other peccadilloes it was to her, and to none other, that Lenin committed his most urgent directives concerning main policy for the Bolsheviks once the smoke of the February Revolution had cleared over Petrograd.

Lenin's sporadic attempts at establishing closer relations with the revolutionaries in Russia could hardly satisfy his appetite for action, and with the ample time now at his disposal he resumed his favourite pastime of reading. In the library of Zurich University he studied for the first time the philosophy of Hegel – the founder of 'dialectics'. He made copious notes and marginal comments out of which Soviet philosophers have striven to reconstruct an original Leninist philosophy.

At this time Lenin also began to take a greater interest in the international socialist movement and, in particular, the Swiss. The magic of his arguments and the force of his personality did not serve him as well among them as they did among his Russian followers. At an international conference of anti-war socialists which gathered in September 1915 in the village of Zimmerwald near Berne, Lenin found himself heading a small minority whose slogan was civil war between the classes, as opposed to the majority's call for a struggle for peace. In the spring of 1916 Lenin called another conference in the Swiss village of Kienthal, and now an appeal was adopted calling on the proletarians of all belligerent countries either to lay down their arms or to turn them against their governments. From Lenin's remarks on the internationally-minded socialists, it is clear he reckoned little with their effective support or with their acceptance of his leadership.

In 1916 he was already forty-six and the course of world events was not going according to his predictions. He had squandered his time and his extraordinary abilities in the futile attempt at establishing his own, subservient, Russian revolutionary party. He had lost the esteem of people such as Bukharin, who could enhance the moral reputation of the Bolsheviks. Was he perhaps resigned to the fate of an obscure propagandist who would never reap the harvest he had sown? When addressing a conference of young socialists in Zurich in January 1917, he told them that although possibly people of his generation might not see the decisive struggle for socialism, they, the young, would take part in it and win a glorious victory. Evidently Lenin expected the revolution to begin outside Russia, in the advanced industrialised countries. As for

Russia, Lenin's pessimism was not misplaced. The arrest and banishment of the Bolshevik Duma deputies resulted in total disorder in the Bolshevik lines. Local committees were working more or less underground in Petrograd, in a few provincial centres, and among the workers and sailors of Kronstadt. But most of these were closely watched by the security police who had infiltrated their agents into them. Lenin's propaganda to the workers in Russia was concerned more with denouncing any compromise with other socialist parties than with calling directly for insurrection against the Tsar.

In the last months before the February Revolution Lenin turned his thoughts to reorganising his activities on an international scale. Thus he despatched Inessa Armand ('la maitresse de Lénine', as she was invariably described in the reports of the French secret service) to France to spread defeatist propaganda. In Inessa he met with a type of woman very different from Krupskaya. Her revolutionary activism was not, as in the case of Krupskaya, derivative from Lenin's personality and she could stand her ground, sometimes in sharp exchanges with him. Lenin's emotional attachment to her was probably the strongest in his life, after his respectful love for his mother. Inessa followed him on his triumphal return to Russia and he mourned openly her untimely death from typhus in 1920.

The thought that the war might end without giving birth to the socialist revolution obsessed Lenin, particularly in the second half of 1916 and up to the outbreak of the rising in Petrograd and the abdication of the Tsar. Contrary to anything his widow asserted later, Lenin had little reason for believing in the imminence of revolution, in Russia or elsewhere. It was, therefore, with elation and incredulity that he looked up when an Austrian Social Democrat and admirer, Bronsky, broke into his room announcing the fall of the Tsarist regime.

The February Revolution

The strain of modern war, for which Russia was not prepared, the political pressure of the opposition parties, which increasingly used personal criticism as a weapon against the Imperial family on account of their close relationship with the notorious Rasputin, the denunciations by these parties of the government's inefficiency, and indeed the inefficiency itself, proved too great a weight on the absolutist structure which had lasted 300 years. When in February 1917 the demonstrations of the type that had occurred a year before got out of hand and were augmented by mutinous troops from the ill-

Left: Demoralised Russian troops in full flight, July 1917

49

disciplined Petrograd garrison, the Tsarist government lost its head and let the reins of power slip into the hands of a Provisional Government. The Tsar, isolated from all his supporters, did not oppose the revolutionary government and abdicated. His brother and heir, Grand Duke Michael, refused the crown unless it were given to him by a Constituent Assembly, elected on the basis of universal suffrage. The Provisional Government immediately enacted a number of liberal and permissive laws, abolishing the police of all kinds and replacing them by a people's militia. Under these conditions of complete freedom of speech and therefore of propaganda during time of war, the country rapidly fell into a state of total anarchy, which was to give Lenin and his small party their opportunity.

The next days after the news of the Revolution Lenin spent in collecting and piecing together the bits of often garbled information which agencies were sending abroad. His reaction to the news was noticeably different from that of the other revolutionary groups. In his telegrams to Madame Kollontay in Sweden and in a series of articles entitled 'Letters from Afar', Lenin made the point again and again that although the fall of the Tsarist regime was a welcome event, the formation of a Provisional Government including Prince Lvov (a prince!) and the socialist patriot Kerensky showed once again that the struggle for which the workers of Petrograd had shed their blood brought victory only to the bourgeoisie.

Perhaps it was the atmosphere of festivity and mutual forgiveness among the revolutionaries in Switzerland that induced Lenin to emphasise to his followers in Scandinavia, who were nearest to the centre of events, that on no account should any joint action or, God forbid, alliance be contemplated between the Bolsheviks and the other Russian socialist parties. In 1917, on receiving the first issues of the Bolshevik paper *Pravda,* Lenin was furious at the concessions being made to mass emotionalism: now the shackles of the Tsarist regime have fallen, they were saying, the Russian giant will surprise the world by a speedy victory over its external enemies and by building up a society worthy of the dignity of man. For Lenin 'February 1917' was a bourgeois revolution in which the Russian middle classes had used the proletariat to get rid of the semi-feudal autocracy and then installed their own state-power behind a smokescreen of

Left: One of the most intriguing figures of the revolutionary movement — Alexander Helphand, alias Parvus (on left). A wealthy Russo-German Social Democrat, he was influential in guiding German policy towards support of the Bolsheviks. He is shown with fellow-revolutionaries Trotsky and Lev Deich in 1906

51

democratic institutions. He nonetheless recognised that in this 'freest country in the world' which Russia had become the prospect for his own plans was shining bright.

Lenin's journey to the Finland Station

The wildest projects for a quick return to Russia were put forward only to be immediately rejected. For some reason, for which no conclusive proof has ever been given, Lenin believed that the Allied powers of the Entente would prevent his return to Russia even if the Provisional Government were not to raise any difficulties. We know that this was not the case for many of the Bolsheviks. Why should restrictions have been applied to Lenin who, for the world at large, was only one of the many Russian revolutionary émigrés? It was at this turning point that to everybody's amazement Lenin decided to return to his homeland via Germany. No other event in his life has raised so much bitter controversy as to the facts. The German government had been aware of Lenin's existence for some time before the beginning of the Russian revolution. Various agents whom the Germans employed to study the political situation had reported Lenin's amazing defeatist theories. Two of them, as was mentioned earlier, managed to impress their German contacts considerably. One was Dr Alexander Helphand, alias Parvus, who had established a research institute in Copenhagen, and who had provided Lenin's agent in Scandinavia, Jacob Haniecki, with a lucrative job in Copenhagen whence he was subsequently deported for blackmarket activities. The other was Keskuela, an Estonian patriot and a former member of the Bolshevik party. Both were political adventurers in the 'grand style' and their contacts and advice were not ignored by the German authorities. Parvus' failure to produce a revolution in Russia early in 1916, and other political setbacks, increased German scepticism about playing too many cards in the political game. But they kept Lenin as a potential weapon for the appropriate moment. It came in March 1917.

Although the Germans knew perfectly well that Lenin had nothing to do directly or indirectly with the fall of Tsarism they immediately saw the limitless possibilities for his defeatist propaganda in the turmoil of revolutionary Russia. The idea of letting Lenin travel through German territory presented itself simultaneously to many people concerned with Russian affairs in Germany. But the most influential was the opinion of the Political Department of the General Staff, which proposed on the suggestion of Parvus the immediate transportation of Lenin either via Sweden or by a special armistice corridor at the front. The Swedish idea seemed the soundest and the most acceptable to Lenin himself. To camouflage

the repatriation of Lenin and Zinoviev a number of other émigrés, some of them without any express defeatist views, were put on the list by Lenin and his advisers and were accepted by the Germans.

The story of Lenin's journey in the 'sealed train' has been told with more or less fanciful details far too many times. Some points, however, should be put on record on the basis of relatively recent research, insofar as they help to explain Lenin's ascent to political influence and finally to political power. Lenin himself not only concealed but distorted the story of his return to Russia and subsequent activities there, even though he never tried to pose as a moralist in political matters. The first step towards his return was taken by the Germans themselves. The Political Department of the German General Staff asked the Foreign Office to provide a certain Georg Sklarz with papers for an important mission to Switzerland. Sklarz stayed for three days to negotiate Lenin's journey. Fritz Platten, a Swiss leftist Social Democrat who was to accompany Lenin to the Russian frontier, wrote in his book about the journey that Lenin put an abrupt end to these talks as soon as he had identified Sklarz as a hyena of disgraceful reputation and an agent of Parvus. But it was the same Platten, who in 1922, previous to his later book, revealed that the negotiations with Sklarz had lasted for three days. Platten wrote then: 'Only after it became clear to Lenin that Ludendorff had a part in this game and that the plan could easily produce a compromising situation for him, did Lenin break off these negotiations.'

It was Platten again who, on his return to Switzerland after chaperoning Lenin's party to the Russian frontier, immediately reported to the German envoy in Berne on the success of the operation and also pointed out to him that compared with other political parties the Bolsheviks were extremely small in number and would need substantial funds provided in the most discreet way in order to build up their activity and influence. The envoy reported the matter to Berlin, and as a result the Foreign Secretary Kühlmann could report to the Kaiser on the 3rd December 1917 that 'it was not until the Bolsheviks had received from us a steady flow of funds through various channels and under different labels that they were in a position to be able to build up their main organ, *Pravda,* to conduct energetic propaganda, and appreciably to extend the originally narrow basis of their party'. It is only relatively recently that these facts have become acceptable, if unpalatable, to many Western historians. The strange thing is that neither Lenin nor his

Left: Distribution of anti-war leaflets and newspapers, early 1917

53

successors ever conceded the simple truth that besides transport facilities he had also been using German money to achieve his political success. Yet the very mention of this arouses the fury of Soviet historians and is denounced as based on forgeries, while all the evidence is there for anyone who wants it.

Even stranger is the attitude of successive German governments to this question. In 1922 the elder German Social Democrat Bernstein asked in the parliament of the Weimar Republic whether it was true that the Kaiser's government had spent something like fifty million marks in support of the Bolshevik revolution. The answer was 'No'.

Perhaps this was because the German government under the Kaiser was never privy to the secret dealings of the Foreign Office and the Political Section of the General Staff, through which such matters were conducted. There is sufficient evidence to show that even the mention of Lenin's name in Foreign Office correspondence was discouraged. Nevertheless, we know from a report from the Foreign Minister Kühlmann to the Kaiser that monies from the German government were 'transferred to the Bolsheviks by different channels and under various labels'. We know of at least some of these channels, operating through Scandinavia at various times in 1917. On the one hand were German secret agents such as the historian Gustav Mayer, the Swiss Social Democrat Karl Moor, and Helphand-Parvus and Keskuela, who were all at one time or another instrumental in establishing contacts and conveying funds to the Bolsheviks in Scandinavia represented by Haniecki, Radek, and Vorovsky.

Lenin, who knew all too well the importance of finance in revolution, could not possibly have remained uninformed of these goings-on, though to be sure the concrete evidence that he did know is not to hand, nor is it likely ever to have existed. Both he and the conspiratorial group of German officials engaged in these dealings were much too conscious of the danger of exposure to have allowed such evidence to be recorded. We must therefore content ourselves with the occasional hints in the German documents and in the memoirs of those involved in this operation.

The trouble is that this relatively minor circumstance removes the heroic element of Lenin's lonely struggle for the liberation of the toiling masses and reduces his historical status as prophet and statesman to that of a successful intriguer and opportunist. By letting his followers rebut what he had called the Russian 'Dreyfus affair', Lenin managed to build up the mythology of the Russian revolution without including any reference to

German assistance. Nevertheless, without it Lenin might never have emerged from the obscurity to which his dogmatism, fractiousness, and unscrupulous use of political intrigue had condemned him for the first forty-seven years of his life.

Lenin travelled with Krupskaya, Inessa Armand, Zinoviev and his family, and a number of lesser figures, strictly observing the rules of extra-territoriality which were laid down in an official document signed by him and counter-signed by Platten and other anti-war socialists, including Lenin's friend Guilbeaux, who later emerged as an ideologist of the Nazi movement. The question remains: did Lenin conclude any oral or written agreement with the German government to follow a certain line of action once in Russia? The record of relations between the German Foreign Ministry and the Bolsheviks is not available, if it exists. We can, however, do no better than let a German diplomat expose at least the fact of German-Bolshevik operations. At the beginning of May 1917 the German Ambassador at Berne, who seems to have been the least discreet of diplomats, instructed Schubert, a subordinate officer on his staff, to write privately to a high official at the Foreign Office and to ask 'whether your Russian connections cover not only Lenin and his group, but also the leading Socialist Revolutionaries . . .' The Ambassador was *extremely* anxious to have this information *as soon as possible,* and asks that you send it by telegram'.

The cabled reply was brief: 'I have no connections with them.' This correspondence and the way it was conducted show how intent the German Foreign Office was on preventing a leak of its contacts with Lenin. Schubert's letter was a breach of the precautionary measures and was filed in the Foreign Ministry archives, due, doubtless, to an oversight. Subsequent reports from agents that Lenin was working satisfactorily and in accordance with 'our expectations' make it plain that both the financial help and an agreement on co-ordinated action between the German government and Lenin had the desired effect.

The actual journey from Switzerland to the Finland Station in Petrograd was relatively uneventful. As the train left the siding in Zurich, a group of 'Social Patriots' interrupted the singing of the 'Internationale' with catcalls and insults such as 'Spies' and 'Traitors'; Lenin himself appears to have man-handled a potential traveller, who was wrongly suspected of being a police agent; another traveller missed the train by a couple of minutes.

Left: February 1917 saw demonstrations in Petrograd. Workers at a cartridge factory demand protection for child labour

Lenin travelled most of the way to Stockholm in a separate compartment with Krupskaya. In her memoirs Krupskaya reports that Lenin was seriously concerned that they might be arrested either at the Russian frontier or on arrival in Petrograd. If this is not a slip of memory it shows how little Lenin knew of conditions at home. The Provisional Government was still adhering to the principle that they had no enemies on the Left. The Bolshevik Party was an established institution with its own press and its own bureau in the Petrograd Soviet. Bolshevik deportees such as the Duma deputies and many others, arrested for sabotage of the war effort, were returning to the capital. They would trouble Lenin more than the thought of the arrest which never came.

After the party had crossed into Finland Lenin was met by Kamenev, who had just been released from banishment in Siberia and had taken over, together with Stalin, the editorship of *Pravda*. The Bolsheviks in Russia, in spite of Lenin's admonitions, had succumbed to the general mood of conciliation prevailing among all the groups and parties which had been in opposition to the Tsarist regime. Accordingly *Pravda* had taken the line that it would support the new government insofar as it was carrying out revolutionary aims. It also took a defencist attitude and gave its blessing to the national effort to save the newly-gained freedom from destruction by German invasion.

Lenin rebuked Kamenev on both points and tried to convince him that the bourgeois revolution could, under the specific circumstances of war and mobilisation in Russia, be immediately transformed into a radical social revolution, provided no opportunity was missed. For his part, Kamenev probably explained to Lenin that the purely defeatist attitude had been an ideological handicap for the party even before the revolution. Now, with an army sworn to allegiance to the Provisional Government and steeped in the idea of a Constituent Assembly, the Bolsheviks would find themselves totally isolated in their defeatism even among the left socialist parties. On the question of an immediate peace, Lenin found it wise to make certain concessions. He admitted that the masses had been so exposed to official and unofficial war propaganda that they really believed that it was in their own interests to win, but by patient, systematic, and unremitting agitation this mood could be changed and the question of an immediate peace then raised.

Left: *Soldiers and students lie in wait for the police. The Tsar's abdication was close at hand—and with it Lenin's opportunity*

Chapter 4
Bolsheviks versus Liberals

Lenin arrived in Russia at a moment when the mood of collective rejoicing and mutual forgiveness was gradually being superseded by the tedium of hearing the same statements and promises being repeated endlessly at higher and higher pitch. The readiness of night porters to fight to the last drop of their blood for an eight-hour night did not arouse greater enthusiasm than the Prime Minister's assurance that the soul of the Russian people was deeply democratic and that they would lead all the other nations into the paradise of total democracy. Yet Lenin quickly understood that he must proceed warily. He first proclaimed himself a strong supporter of a Constituent Assembly which he wanted convened by some magic means within a few days. He accused the government of postponing electoral legislation in order to strengthen the position of the bourgeoisie and to secure the kind of democratic swindle which typified the so-called Western democracies. At the same time he urged an attitude of 'no confidence' towards the Provisional Government, even though they had conceded a degree of political licence which no warfaring country would normally tolerate. In the transitional period before the elections and the convocation of the Constituent Assembly it was the soviets which were to take over what was then called, with some pomp and very little content, 'the total plenitude of power'. Without delay the soviets were expected to carry out the confiscation of private and church estates, to bring an instant end to the war, and to make peace not between bourgeois governments but between the workers of all belligerent countries.

In one respect Bolshevik propaganda remained very cautious. Instead of urging a separate peace it spoke of the international proletariat taking the question of war and peace out of the hands of top-hatted diplomats and of letting the toiling masses themselves decide it by clasping fraternal calloused hands through the barbed-wire

Left: The road to Petrograd — Lenin (with umbrella) in Stockholm in April 1917 on his way back to Russia. Zinoviev is on the far left of the émigrés, with his son whom Lenin wanted to adopt

at the front. Swarms of propagandists with 'mandates' from the Petrograd Soviet journeyed to the front to incite the troops to make direct contact with their class-brethren on the other side and to make partial armistice agreements of their own. They were not always met in a friendly way by the soldiers and were often prevented from getting to the trenches by the local headquarters or an enterprising officer. According to the Bolsheviks such officers were manifesting class interest in the continuation of the war and they must be removed, either by a superior command or by execution in the field. They were, moreover, violating one of the most sacred gains of the revolution, namely, freedom of speech. Thus the fraternisation campaign became one of the main levers used by Lenin to remove the chief obstacle on his way to power—the Russian army.

Lenin openly endorsed fraternisation in his speeches from the strategically-placed balcony of the ballerina Kshesinskaya's small palace and in the columns of *Pravda*. He even quoted supposed orders to German officers to prevent fraternisation. But he did this to give the Russian soldiers the feeling that the enemy was suffering from the same kind of intolerable oppression as they themselves. In fact, the detailed information which is now available on the progress of the fraternisation campaign shows that the German soldiers were well-instructed on how to fraternise, and officers, sometimes in soldiers' uniform, supervised the actual fraternising. Temporary cease-fire agreements were concluded and on the whole kept. Sometimes, however, the agreement was made with the infantry in the trenches only, and Russian artillery would take advantage of the relaxed atmosphere on the German side and open fire. When this happened the infantry would send delegates to the battery threatening to kill the artillery officers in charge.

Perfectly accustomed as he was to public speaking, Lenin soon after returning to Russia found ample opportunity for this activity: on any day of the week one could find a motley crowd hanging around the Kshesinskaya palace in the hope that somebody would titillate their revolutionary passion. He also contributed to *Pravda*, but he concentrated his main effort on organising the party, keeping in touch with the provinces, instructing agitators. The secret contact which Lenin maintained with his friends in Scandinavia was to cause him some anxiety. He wrote in May to his unofficial envoy in Stockholm, Haniecki, that he was worried because 'the promised letter, monies, and parcels have still not arrived'. These items were to come to Lenin from the German General

Right: Russian and German troops fraternise at the front

Staff and Foreign Ministry by way of a German scholar called Gustav Mayer, who was to travel to Stockholm where his totally unsuspicious residence was to be the collection point.

At the end of April a situation arose in which for the first time the Bolsheviks could attempt to implement their programme of insurrection. The Minister of Foreign Affairs, Milyukov, published a diplomatic Note addressed to the Allies, in which he averred that Russia would honour the obligations undertaken by the Tsarist government and that she would defend her rights under the wartime agreements, including control of Constantinople and the Straits. The publication was untimely and irritating for many quarters and in despatching his Note Milyukov certainly earned the jibe that he was a 'god of tactlessness'. Neither Constantinople nor the Straits were in the hands of the Allies nor could Milyukov as a member of the Provisional Government prejudge the attitude to this question which would be taken by the Constituent Assembly. No wonder the opportunity was seized upon by Bolshevik agitators to point out to the soldiers that they were fighting not only for foreign predatory interests but also for those of the Russian bourgeoisie, the main representatives of which, in the Provisional Government, were Guchkov and Milyukov. At exactly the same time the German envoys to Stockholm and Copenhagen reported Guchkov, the Minister of War, and Milyukov as leaders of the extreme war-party in Russia.

The Bolsheviks immediately organised a demonstration in favour of a peace without annexation and indemnities and with the express demand for the expulsion of Guchkov and Milyukov from the government. The demonstration passed quite peacefully and was followed the next day by a counter-demonstration, headed by war-disabled men demanding the continuation of the war to a victorious end. A meeting of the government took place at which Kerensky, the Minister of Justice, took a pronounced anti-Milyukov line which resulted in Milyukov's resignation. Guchkov, who was ill at that time and had not been able to stop the defeatist propaganda and the fraternisation at the front, resigned with him and thus a path was opened for the entry of Socialist deputies from the soviets into the Provisional Government.

No less important was a demonstration instigated by revolutionary agitators in which a regiment came out in support of the so-called peace-party denunciations of Milyukov and Guchkov. General Kornilov, the Commander of the Petrograd garrison, demanded punishment

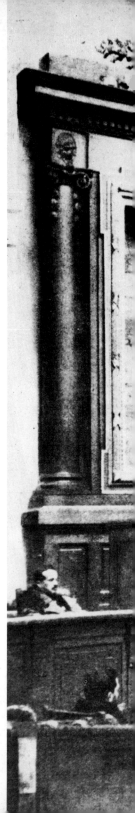

Right: The Duma in session before (inset) and after February 1917. Soldiers replaced deputies, removing the Tsar's picture

of this regiment and insisted that no troops should be so used without his permission. The military section of the Soviet claimed that this was a political action and that in political matters the Petrograd garrison took its orders from the Soviet. The head of the Provisional Government, the weak and conciliatory Prince Lvov, tried to smooth things over, but Kornilov was unyielding and, disgusted by the situation in the capital, demanded to be returned to the army in the field, where he became Commander-in-Chief of the South-Western Front.

The April demonstrations and the support given in the soviets to this kind of harassment of the Provisional Government provoked sharp reaction among liberals, who considered the February Revolution as their own achievement and deplored the political aspirations of the Petrograd Soviet as both pretentious and disruptive. The President of the last Duma summoned a meeting of all available members of past Dumas to discuss the serious situation created by this evident bifurcation of power. This was possibly the first attempt to create a body representative of Russian public opinion to which the government would be in some way answerable, and from which it might derive some measure of the authority without which it was looked upon merely as a gathering of gifted, well-meaning usurpers.

At the meeting, on 27th April, the right-wing deputy Shulgin accused Lenin of being a conspirator and attacked the government for tolerating subversion. The Menshevik Tseretelli retorted that on the contrary Lenin was a mere propagandist and that everybody now enjoyed the right of free expression. He went on to say that if the majority of the bourgeoisie held Shulgin's views, then he, Tseretelli, would have no choice but to accept Lenin's dictatorship. But Tseretelli did not believe this to be the case, and he could thus collaborate with the government. Tseretelli's defence earned him little gratitude from Lenin, who lectured him pedantically for revisionism.

In spite of the Provisional Government's permissiveness and Tseretelli's dubious casuistry Lenin's political position remained precarious during May 1917. The agitation for an immediate end to the war was having a powerful effect among the armed forces and Lenin did not want anybody to appropriate this powerful weapon. It would help to destroy the Russian army not only as a fighting force in the war but also as a potential defender of the Provisional Government.

By the end of May Bolshevik anti-war propaganda had already penetrated deep into the body of the army in the field. The March declaration of the Petrograd Soviet, in which all demands for annexation and reparations were repudiated, was exploited in Lenin's propaganda to mean that the troops should forthwith lay down their arms. The message was conveyed by various means: there was the special Bolshevik newspaper 'The Soldiers' Pravda' or the 'Trench Pravda' which set out these ideas simply enough for any intelligent NCO to understand; there was the oral propaganda to which troops in the rear, in hospitals, and on leave, were systematically subjected; there was the German-produced press, thrown over the barbed wire and completely in tune with Bolshevik propaganda. And there was not least an uneasy awareness among the men at the front that soldiers like themselves were controlling the government in Petrograd, while they had to submit to the orders of officers who had been appointed by the old regime and who very often made no secret of their hostility to the innovations of the past few weeks.

Kerensky attains supreme power

By the end of April the disintegration of the army had become so advanced that even the Provisional Government realised that the foundations of army morale, loyalty to the Tsar and the defence of the Fatherland, must be replaced by a new ideology to capture the imagination of the troops. The first two months had shown them the great capacity possessed by Kerensky, the Minister of Justice, for changing the mood of a demoralised crowd through sheer rhetoric. He replaced Guchkov as Minister of War and later became head of the government as well, thus gathering in his hands a concentration of nominal power which even the Emperor had hardly ever possessed.

Kerensky and Lenin had never met and had probably seen each other only once in the middle of June at the First All-Russian Congress of the Soviets. For revolutionary zeal Kerensky need yield nothing to Lenin, and both of them firmly believed that society could be reorganised only by means of state-power. Lenin, however, possessed a remarkable ability to grasp and correctly evaluate political situations, an ability notably lacking in his chief adversary. On the other hand, Kerensky's histrionic and oratorical talents far outstripped Lenin's. His personality made a colossal impact on the masses. He could speak only without notes, as if possessed by a force which made him behave like an epileptic, a victim of that sacred disease from which many founders of religious and mass movements have suffered. He often lost consciousness after an impassioned speech, but that only added force in the eyes

Left: Rodzianko, President of the Duma (sitting), and Kerensky, Minister of Justice in the new Provisional Government, the main Right and Left personalities of the February Revolution

of the masses, who were mesmerised by his eloquence.

As soon as he became Minister of War Kerensky decided to attack Bolshevik influence at its roots, and he undertook a rapid tour of the front. His appearance was highly successful virtually everywhere, and the revolutionary army paid him the hysterical tribute to which he was already accustomed. The main theme of his harangues was that the Russian soldier had always been unsurpassed in his readiness to die for the right cause. But under the Tsarist regime he had been driven into battle by his officers, threatened by whip and pistol. Now, however, the first country to proclaim the ideals of social democracy was asking the Russian soldier to sacrifice his life for a better future, not only of his own country but of the whole of humanity.

Despite Lenin's interest in the decomposition of the army he did not copy Kerensky by paying visits to the front. He remained entrenched in Petrograd and purveyed his propaganda to the 200,000 troops of the Petrograd garrison and the naval base of nearby Kronstadt. The Kronstadt Soviet, in particular, became the setting for trying out various techniques of rapid subversion. Kronstadt was the only military establishment in which Bolsheviks had had an underground cell before the February Revolution. Now it had formed, more or less democratically, a soviet of its own, the Soviet of Soldiers, Sailors, and Workers. Mutinous sailors had at the outbreak of the revolution committed atrocities, shooting or drowning many of their own officers.

The Kronstadt Soviet had a wider spectrum than most, with a strong anarchist element and a good number of Socialist Revolutionaries. When the Provisional Government, in an attempt to save the unfortunate officers, demanded their transfer to Petrograd prisons for immediate investigation, the Soviet passed a resolution categorically refusing obedience to the Provisional Government and declaring that it would take orders from the Petrograd Soviet only.

Lenin's line of action had been demonstrably successful. On the one hand this act of open mutiny at Kronstadt, if it passed unchallenged, would serve as an example to other units. On the other hand the Petrograd Soviet, which Lenin urged to seize power from the very beginning of his campaign, was forced to take action which would show that it not merely controlled but in certain respects dominated the activities of the Provisional Government. This time, however, the Executive Committee of the Petrograd Soviet showed a certain solidarity with the

Left: Kerensky (on the left) takes the salute. A moderate socialist, he dominated the Provisional Government for six months

Provisional Government. A right-wing Menshevik called Skobelev was sent to Kronstadt, where he came to an understanding with the Soviet, and the Provisional Government's authority was formally restored.

Lenin was not discouraged. For him the main thing was the close contact of the Bolshevik organisation in Kronstadt with the Bolshevik Central Committee in Petrograd. He would need the Kronstadt sailors for armed support as soon as the opportunity for an armed insurrection in the capital presented itself. He had not long to wait. After the resignation of the 'Imperialist' ministers Guchkov and Milyukov, the Provisional Government took in representatives of the Petrograd Soviet with more or less moderate socialist convictions. Without dropping his demand for 'All power to the soviets!' Lenin concentrated his attacks on these 'despicable socialists' who had been tempted into office in the Provisional Government. The socialists had four representatives in the government whereas the other ten members belonged to the left wing of the liberal ex-Duma parties. Lenin demanded the resignation of the 'ten capitalist ministers'. At that moment it proved to be poor tactics.

At the beginning of June, after much persuasion, certain units of the South-Western Front showed readiness to obey the order for a powerful offensive on the Austrian Front. The German High Command had purposely refrained from taking advantage of the falling morale of the Russian army to go over to an offensive. They feared that a successful penetration into Russia might provoke a reawakening of patriotic feeling and generate resistance, thereby impeding the mobility of their forces as a whole and thus weakening their position on the Western Front. The Russian offensive began with selected shocktroops, composed of volunteers from the front, university students who wanted to serve revolutionary Russia, and even a battalion of women who wanted to put male deserters to shame. This force broke the thin Austrian forward defence, captured a number of prisoners, took the towns of Tarnopol and Galich, and created a situation in which a major offensive might have developed. For almost a fortnight the Russian press, except for that of the Bolsheviks, wrote deliriously of the heroic achievements of the Free and Democratic new Russian Army. Soon, however, it became obvious that the initial blow would not be followed by a major offensive, because the orders to advance were disobeyed by supporting units.

The Germans organised their counter-offensive with a vengeance and the units which had refused to fight in the Kerensky offensive fled under the least pressure, committing unspeakable outrages in their flight, burning down towns and villages, raping and killing the civilian popu-

lation. The Commander of the South-Western Front, General Kornilov, demanded an immediate abandonment of all offensive operations on his front, and special powers for the restoration of discipline, including the death penalty for cowardice in the face of the enemy.

The news of the débâcle was music to Lenin's ears. He had just suffered humiliation at the hands of the right-wing socialist parties of the Soviet. At the general meeting of the First All-Russian Congress of Soviets, Tseretelli had declared that there was no single party prepared at this time to assume the 'plenitude of power'. Lenin had risen and shouted from his place: 'There is such a party!', only to be greeted by the mocking laughter of the Congress.

While the moderate applause of the Bolsheviks could not give much encouragement to Lenin, the confusion among the coalition socialists spurred him into a more daring and adventurous exercise. On 9th June the walls of the Petrograd garrison were plastered with a Bolshevik appeal to the soldiers to join the workers in a peaceful demonstration the next day. The appeal claimed that the Provisional Government with ten bourgeois ministers in its ranks was falling increasingly under the influence of landowners and capitalists. Instead of defending the conquests of the revolution the government tolerated and indeed incited the irresponsible bacchanalia of the counter-revolutionaries. All power must be transferred to the soviets; all orders for discipline in the ranks of the forces must be annulled: 'It is time to put an end to the war! Let the Soviet declare conditions of peace based on justice! Neither separate peace with Wilhelm nor secret agreements with the French and English capitalists! Bread! Peace! Freedom!'

The moderate socialists at the Soviet Congress moved a resolution requesting the Bolshevik Party to cancel their demonstration. In spite of the fact that certain non-Bolshevik deputies including Martov tended to defend the right of a socialist party to call their followers into the streets, the Bolsheviks resolved to submit to the mood of the Congress and they suspended for three days their appeal for demonstrations. The next day *Pravda* appeared with an enormous blank space on the front page where the appeal for a 'spontaneous' demonstration was to have been printed. But the preparations for the demonstration, described by Tseretelli as the '10th of June conspiracy', had gone far and could be reactivated at any time. Tseretelli's accusation provoked a violent reaction among the Bolsheviks and some of their supporters in the Executive Committee of the Congress. To placate the democratic sensibilities which had been affronted by

Left: Metalworkers demonstrate in their Sunday best, May 1917

69

Tseretelli's phrase, the Congress decided to hold a peaceful demonstration on the 18th with the participation of all party groups including the Bolsheviks, to show the support of the Petrograd proletariat and garrison for the general policy of the Congress. The Bolsheviks, who had had everything ready for the 10th, had an obvious advantage over the majority parties, which had not been campaigning in the factories and barracks. The prevalence of posters with Bolshevik slogans such as 'Down with the ten capitalist ministers!' and the mood of the crowds in the streets suggested substantial support for any violent political action which the Bolsheviks might choose to start. It is possible that the events in the capital on the 18th June would have had wider repercussions had not the ill-fated Kerensky offensive started the very same day, creating for a short time the illusion that the revolutionary army under the guidance of the Provisional Government could work miracles at the front.

But worse things were in store for the government. The unity of the coalition and its readiness to compromise proved to be very superficial. On two major issues of internal policy the right faction, which answered to the Constitutional Democrat Party (Kadets), and the left, which answered to the Soviet, were far from understanding each other. The fall of Tsarism had strengthened the demand of national minorities for far-reaching autonomy and in more than one case for outright independence. Throughout the war some of them received encouragement and material help from the Germans. In particular the Germans wanted to secure a foothold in the Ukraine and were prepared to add to the Russian government's troubles by exacerbating its relations with the Ukrainian nationalist militants. At the outbreak of the February Revolution Ukrainian extremist nationalists built up their own organisation (the Central *Rada* or Council in Kiev) which attempted to take over the administration of the country.

At the time of the collapse of the Kerensky offensive, the Kadet ministers in his government resigned in protest against an agreement made by a government deputation to the Kiev *Rada* granting the latter the status of a national government. This agreement pre-empted a fundamental prerogative of the future Constituent Assembly which was to decide on the structure of the Russian state.

The other major issue on which the Kadet party could not agree with the socialists in the government was that of agrarian policy. The socialist minority wanted to enact a prohibition on all dealings in land, on the understanding that the Constituent Assembly would proclaim the nationalisation of all land, and dealings at this time

would therefore only confuse matters for later. The Kadets were indignant at this pre-emption of the decisions of the Constituent Assembly and at the 'gross infringement of property rights' implied.

The July Days

The ministerial crisis of the night of 2nd/3rd July had still to be reported in the press when, on the morning of the 3rd, the Executive Committee of the Soviet received news that unidentified agitators were inciting workers and Red militia, as well as units of the garrison, to come out that day to demonstrate for a seizure of power by the soviets. This was followed by the appearance of a small Bolshevik deputation headed by Stalin, who declared that the Bolshevik Party was doing its best to avert a demonstration by sending its delegates to the factories and barracks. Stalin even asked for his declaration to be included in the minutes of the Executive Committee meeting. Tseretelli recalls a remark made on this occasion by the chairman of the Soviet, Chkheidze: 'Well, this clarifies the situation to a certain extent. Peaceful people do not need to have their peaceful intentions recorded in minutes. It looks very much as if we will have to deal with this so-called spontaneous demonstration which the Bolsheviks will join on the excuse that the masses cannot be left without guidance.'

This point is of fundamental historical importance. Soviet historians, diligently fulfilling the task entrusted to them by the Party, never tire of providing proof that neither Lenin nor the Bolshevik Central Committee had anything to do with preparing the rising of 3rd-6th July. Lenin himself had left the capital on the eve of the demonstrations to recuperate in Finland from nervous tension which caused him headaches and sleeplessness. According to official Soviet accounts there was no need for the Bolsheviks to embark on an armed adventure at that precise moment. Lenin was still confident, they insist, that state power would sooner or later slip without violence into the hands of the soviets which themselves would become predominantly Bolshevik through the rapid increase of class consciousness among the workers and soldiers. The discontent of the masses which caused the demonstration was not the result of propaganda but a natural reaction of the soldiers against 'draconian measures' applied or proposed by the Provisional Government.

Relations between the Petrograd garrison and the Provisional Government were certainly unsatisfactory,

Left: General Polovtsev with troops recalled from the front by Kerensky to combat the Bolsheviks in Petrograd in July

71

but not precisely in the way implied by this view. At its very inception the Provisional Government committed a suicidal act by promising not to remove from the capital the units which had mutinied in February, and that meant the whole of the Petrograd garrison. When soldiers at the front protested with indignation against this privilege of the Petrograd garrison, the Petrograd soldiers' representatives agreed to send companies to the front in rotation. In spite of this, the average soldier continued to regard his position as impregnable and refused to co-operate. The fear of provoking mutinous outbreaks restrained the military authorities from applying legal sanctions in cases of disobedience by individual soldiers or whole units.

The Bolsheviks were of course strongly opposed to the rota-system because they hoped to find in the garrison the necessary force for their seizure of power. It is not surprising therefore that the First Machine-gun Regiment, which was due to leave for the front on 4th July, came out in the streets on the evening of 3rd July, demanding the expulsion of capitalist ministers from the government and immediate measures for the conclusion of a democratic peace. The Bolshevik Central Committee also got in touch with Kronstadt to arrange for support by naval ratings.

The route the demonstration was to take was past the Kshesinskaya palace and from there to the Tauride palace, the former seat of the Duma, where now the soviet organisations were centred. Lenin was called back from his retreat in Finland and the Kronstadt forces were called out to join the demonstrators with arms and artillery. With customary Bolshevik duplicity two members of the Central Committee addressed the mob, appealing for an end to the demonstration and a return to barracks. They were met with shouts of 'Down with them!' and 'All power to the soviets!' The Bolshevik Central Committee decided, as Chkheidze had predicted, to organise the 'spontaneous' demonstration.

Lenin was back in the city early in the morning of the 4th when the demonstration was launched again, this time on a much larger scale, but he remained in the background in the Kshesinskaya palace and 'as a precaution' did not stay the night of the 4th/5th July at home but at the flat of Alliluev, the future father-in-law of Stalin.

Right: The July uprising—a large crowd scatters under fire

Chapter 5
The October Revolution

Lenin's behaviour in the July days differs essentially from his tactics and utterances during the October coup. In July the Bolsheviks tried to harness the energy of feeling which they themselves generated, rather as had happened in 1905 in Moscow. In October Lenin was less concerned with the mood of the masses and more attentive to that of his own party, which must seize power largely with its own resources.

The government was regularly ridiculed by Lenin for gross ineptitude and castigated by him for protecting the bourgeoisie at the expense of the workers and peasants. His most searing attacks, however, were reserved, as had always been the case, for the socialists who co-operated in the Provisional Government. Why didn't they order the immediate confiscation of all bank and trust properties? Why didn't they take over control of coal and metal supplies, even at the cost of increased economic disruption? All their false promises to the people were made out of the base wish to retain their position of illusory power. And by these methods of delaying socialist measures the Mensheviks and the Socialist Revolutionaries were, in Lenin's caustic judgment, no less than traitors to the Revolution. Clearly the lesson from all this was not only that all power should be transferred to the soviets, but that those who had by their treacherous behaviour undermined the cause of the proletariat at a time when the fall of Tsarism had made it possible to advance it, must be eliminated and silenced in the soviets.

The July manifestations had ended in a complete fiasco. The Soviet of Soldiers' and Workers' Deputies, whose headquarters were in the Tauride palace, was beleaguered by Red Guards (the armed workers' militia), Kronstadt sailors and soldiers, and units of the Petrograd garrison, demanding that the Soviet declare itself sole authority in Russia, that is, to overthrow the Provisional Government. Instead, the Soviet asked for the intervention of troops faithful to the Provisional Government.

Left: Lenin in hiding. Clean-shaven and bewigged he escaped arrest by the Provisional Government and fled to Finland

Detachments were sent from the front to relieve the Soviet.

The newspapers were full of arguments about who had started the July events. In view of the large numbers of armed people of various political allegiances demonstrating in a confined space the question was not realistic. The Bolsheviks claimed that the rising had been suppressed by right-wing 'Black Hundred' forces. But perhaps the most philosophical and honest assessment of the incident was given by Maxim Gorky, himself something of a Bolshevik:

'I am not a detective. I do not know who is most guilty in this nauseating drama. I have no intention of justifying adventurers. I hate and despise people who excite the dark instincts of the masses . . . I think that a German provocation of the events of 4th July is quite a possibility . . . I consider the main cause of the drama to be not the Leninists, nor the Germans, nor the provocateurs and secret counter-revolutionaries, but a much more evil and powerful enemy – sluggish Russian stupidity.'

The suppression of the 'July rising' had a critical effect on Lenin's position in Russia. It so happened that in the absence of Kerensky and at a moment when liaison between ministries was particularly difficult, the Minister of Justice Pereverzev issued to the press an announcement that criminal proceedings would be taken against Lenin and a number of other persons on a charge of maintaining contact and receiving monies from the German government. News of the impending story spread like wildfire through the Petrograd garrison. The behaviour of the Bolsheviks during the campaign for a peaceful but armed demonstration in favour of an immediate takeover of power by the Soviet appeared against the background of these accusations in a somewhat new light, and enthusiasm for Lenin sagged drastically.

Pereverzev's revelations were to appear in the press on 5th July. On the 4th, however, later in the evening, Stalin rushed to the Soviet and implored Chkheidze, the chairman of the Soviet, to intervene so that the base and groundless slander against the honour of the Bolshevik leaders should not appear the next day. Chkheidze's moral authority was such that neither the socialist nor non-socialist press carried Pereverzev's announcement and evidence. There was one exception, the newspaper *Zhivoe Slovo* (The Living Word), which printed it in full.

The capture of the Kshesinskaya palace by loyal government troops proved unnecessary. Its occupants had fled by the 5th, leaving behind their printing equipment. **81** ▷

Right: Lenin returns to Petrograd to direct the revolution. In the middle of October he announced: 'The time is fully ripe'

'Ten days that shook the world'

The American journalist John Reed thus entitled his account of the seizure of power. Lenin wrote the preface recommending its publication and making it the classic interpretation of his political victory. By September 1917 the Bolsheviks, with their slogan 'Land, Peace, and Bread!', had secured majorities in the Petrograd and Moscow Soviets. In October Lenin declared: 'The Bolsheviks must seize power immediately', but it was Trotsky, president of the Petrograd Soviet, who was to plan and execute the coup. On 23rd October the troops of the Petrograd garrison acknowledged the Soviet as sole power, and on the 25th the Peter and Paul Fortress with its arsenal went over to the Soviet. That night the seizure of the Winter Palace (romanticised by a Soviet painter (**right**)) took place. The Provisional Government, intimidated by a blank shot from the cruiser *Aurora* (**below**), refused to use force in its own defence. Five soldiers, one sailor, and no defenders were killed

Lenin had also moved, cautiously heeding a tip-off from no less well-placed a person than the Assistant Minister of Justice, one Karinsky. Starting with a pamphlet on the very next day the Bolshevik press, under an array of changing mastheads made necessary by the government's ban on them, faced the charge of complicity with the Germans. Lenin defended himself. His denial is categoric. No Bolsheviks ever received any monies from any Germans. The whole thing was a frame-up by the counter-revolutionaries, hiding behind the screen of democratic hypocrisy embodied in the Provisional Government which, according to him, had at last found its Dreyfus. He announced that he would take the slanderers to court, but when the Provisional Government issued a warrant for his arrest, as well as for the arrest of other persons named in the charge, Lenin not only gave up the idea of accusing them of slander but refused to appear before a court under the Provisional Government, on the grounds that he could expect to get only 'class justice'. It was, moreover, not for him to make it so easy for the bourgeois government to deprive the proletariat of its leadership.

Lenin and Zinoviev went into hiding together in Finland first on a small island off the Finnish coast, near the Finnish-Russian border, then in a comfortable flat in Helsinki itself, under the protection of the local police chief, a Bolshevik sympathiser. From the relative security of Finland, then engaged in a political struggle for its total independence from new-born 'free Russia', Lenin continued to protest against the slander with ever-increasing shrillness of vituperation and decrease of argument. The German government was no less alarmed by the revelations in Petrograd than were the Bolsheviks themselves. The German Ministry of Foreign Affairs ordered Helphand-Parvus to issue a denial of ever having supported Lenin and to swear it before a public notary. The press department was instructed to fight the rumours by every available means.

Lenin's decision to go underground and not to appear in court to clear himself seems to have puzzled the Bolshevik leadership. At the Sixth Party Congress which took place in August without Lenin both Kamenev and Stalin made ambiguous statements in which they at best admitted that only with certain guarantees could Lenin and Zinoviev surrender to the authorities. In fact, much of what Lenin was writing in defence of his decision never reached his readers. Bolshevik papers were closed one after the other and although they reappeared the next day under another name, Lenin hardly had time to react to

Left: The loyal women's battalion – Kerensky's last supporters

the latest events in his articles because of difficulties of communication from his hideout.

Nevertheless he continued to bombard the Central Committee with letters intended for publication in which he denounced the rumour-mongers who supported the monstrous, base, and perfidious slander about his contacts with the Germans. In the meantime, both the government and the Soviet had established committees to investigate the case against Lenin. The government committee was headed by the same Assistant Minister of Justice Karinsky who had tipped Lenin off. But the investigations petered out in the general confusion which engulfed the Provisional Government.

From his hideout in Finland Lenin directed the Finnish Bolshevik Smilga to set up a channel of illegal communication and transport from Sweden to Russia. But his main concern remained the internal situation in Russia. The firm stand which the Petrograd Soviet took in July forced the Bolsheviks to drop the slogan 'All power to the soviets' and to demand instead the total break of the revolutionary toiling masses with the majority parties in the soviets. Lenin now advocated a direct onslaught against the Provisional Government by the Bolshevik party.

The Kornilov affair
In the meantime the political force of the revolution in Russia continued to take its course, barely affected by tactical vacillations inside the Bolshevik party. Plainly something was needed to strengthen the authority of the Provisional Government in the country at large. This could perhaps be achieved either by regular armed forces, which were still at least formally under an oath of allegiance to the Provisional Government, or by special armed detachments under the party control of SRs and Mensheviks, just as the Red Guards of Petrograd were under the control of the Central Committee of the Bolshevik party. The latter plan was studiously avoided by the parties in question as it would have meant a preparation for civil war, and civil war was exactly what they hoped to avoid by convening the Constituent Assembly, eventually elected in accordance with a very democratic polling system. The first solution, to appeal to the armed forces at the front to strengthen the Provisional Government, was not by any means an easy alternative. Only a disciplined army would provide such support. The Commander-in-Chief, General Kornilov, made a desperate effort to obtain from the Provisional Government recognition of the dignity and authority of officers. He proposed the restoration of the death-penalty at the front and in the rear for disobedience, incitement, open mutiny,

looting, and marauding. By now the Provisional Government was dominated by a triumvirate consisting of Kerensky, Nekrasov, and Tereshchenko who, although they belonged to different parties and were of immensely different social background, were bound together by fraternal allegiance to the same political Masonic lodge. These three played cat-and-mouse with the Commander-in-Chief for about six weeks, promising reforms but doing nothing. Such dilatory tactics only led to an open conflict between Kerensky and Kornilov. When the latter was dismissed the army was doomed to total disintegration.

None of this went unnoticed by the Bolsheviks in Petrograd. In the absence of Lenin, Stalin published a number of articles at the beginning of August attacking the idea of possible co-operation between the government and the army command in order to restore discipline and make the enormous armies at the front operational once again. Lenin learned of the new imbroglio only after the dismissal of Kornilov. He certainly approved the formation of a Military Revolutionary Committee by the Petrograd Soviet which, under the chairmanship of a 17-year-old SR, consisted predominantly of Bolsheviks or sympathisers. But like many others who were misled by Kerensky's sanguine attacks on Kornilov, Lenin feared that the Kornilov mutiny would lead to a compromise between Bolsheviks and the Kerensky government in order to avert a military dictatorship: 'We shall fight but we will fight Kornilov just as the troops of Kerensky do, but we do not lend our support to Kerensky. On the contrary we shall expose his weakness.'

Lenin himself soon realised that his fear of a lack of principled behaviour on the part of the Bolshevik Central Committee was unfounded. The Central Committee, where for the first time Stalin played a prominent role, were in complete accord with Lenin on this point. Kerensky's denunciation of his Commander-in-Chief as a rebel, which surprised Kornilov no less than anybody else, tended to convince the lower army ranks of the existence of a widespread counter-revolutionary officers' conspiracy, which threatened the 'conquests of the revolution'. With glee Lenin wrote in those days: 'The peaceful hopes of the petty bourgeoisie for a coalition with the bourgeoisie proper, for an understanding with it, for the possibility of awaiting in peace and dignity the Constituent Assembly which would meet very soon, all this is being shattered by the progress of the revolution in a merciless, cruel, and irrevocable way. The Kornilov affair was the last cruel lesson, a lesson on the grand scale,

Left: *Petrograd workers with a captured armoured car. 'Lt. Schmidt' was an officer who had led a naval mutiny in 1905*

integrating thousands and thousands of small lessons in the deception of workers and peasants by capitalists and landowners, lessons in the deception of soldiers by officers, etc., etc.'

The documents of the period and subsequent events bear out Lenin's contentions completely. It is remarkable that at the very moment when according to him the Bolsheviks were nearing the point at which they could easily seize power they experienced a certain uneasiness, which gradually developed into opposition to Lenin inside the Bolshevik party. The greatest threat to Lenin's revolution at that moment, a threat he tried to avert even before returning to Petrograd from voluntary exile in Finland, was, in his view, the wavering inside the Bolshevik party itself. This danger became apparent in the readiness of the Bolshevik Central Committee to take part in a 'Democratic Conference' and in a subsequent Pre-Parliament which was to give something like parliamentary support for the Provisional Government. The Bolshevik Central Committee actually agreed to send a delegation headed by Trotsky, who had, with a small group of followers, joined the Bolshevik party at the very moment Lenin went into hiding in July. But Trotsky took part in the Pre-Parliament merely by reading a declaration in which the Bolsheviks refused all co-operation, even that of a legal opposition to the Provisional Government. He then proudly led the walk-out of the Bolshevik delegates, for which he earned Lenin's unstinting praise.

From about the middle of September Lenin's messages from Finland became daily more shrill and bellicose. Bolshevik successes in the soviet elections in Petrograd and Moscow, which brought Trotsky to the head of the Petrograd Soviet, appeared to Lenin as one more sign that the time had come for a violent end to the present 'shameful regime' and for the seizure of power by the Petrograd Soviet. One of the most typical outbursts of Lenin's fighting mood is an article he wrote on 29th September, entitled in his *Works* 'The Crisis is Ripe', though part of it has never been found or printed. 'We are gambling,' he said, 'with the whole future of the Bolshevik revolution. The honour of the entire party has been put in question. The future of the socialist world revolution is at risk. An armed rising against the Provisional Government is imperative.' Lenin accused the Central Committee of wanting to postpone a rising until the Second All-Russian Congress of Soviets. 'The victory of such a rising is in the bag for the Bolsheviks. It could happen in Petersburg, Moscow, and the Baltic fleet. We

Right: Trained agitators organised factory workers into armed battalions. Bolshevik agents also stirred up the peasants

have slogans which will secure for us the support of a general peasant rising against this government which protects the landowners against peasant riots. The Bolsheviks are in a majority in the country.' In protest against its procrastinations and its cutting of his articles for the Bolshevik press, Lenin resigned from the Central Committee, 'retaining the freedom to agitate at the lower levels of the party and at the Party Congress. For my ultimate conviction is that if we wait for the Congress of Soviets we shall miss the right moment and bring about the ruin of the revolution.'

Lenin's return from Finland
It is astonishing that in spite of the fact that many leading Bolsheviks maintained personal contact with Lenin and that his movements were recorded by many party members we are in the dark about the exact date of his return to Petrograd. When the question was raised at a conference of Soviet historians in 1966 by one of his secretaries who testified to having given him shelter in the last days of September, a prominent party ideologist, Pospelov, declared that although such personal testimonies were important and welcome, the consensus of the Party, according to which Lenin returned to Petrograd only a fortnight later, should not be disregarded. In the same speech this mentor of Soviet historians made it clear that notes and entries in the diaries of Lenin's secretaries were the patrimony of the Party and the nation and access to them depended on the approval of the Central Committee of the Party.

The point is not without interest. Had Lenin spent a whole month in Petrograd before the rising of 25th October (now celebrated on 7th November in the new calendar), the resistance of his followers to his plans for revolutionary violence would have much greater significance than if it had come only at the last moment, after his return on 10th October when he had no time to persuade every member of the Central Committee. According to the evidence it appears probable that Lenin was already on the spot by the end of September. In any case the tone of his communication to the Central Committee quoted above, 'The Crisis is Ripe', clearly demonstrates a profound disagreement between Lenin and those who still hoped to avoid civil war.

The opposition to Lenin's demand for an immediate rising had' various motives. The reports Bolshevik emissaries gave of the prevailing mood in the Petrograd garrison showed that most of the soldiers were likely to remain neutral in the event of a clash between the government and the Bolsheviks. Much depended, they said, on whether an appeal to join an anti-government

rising was issued by the next Congress of Soviets or only by the Bolshevik party. In fact, a year later Zinoviev was to point out how much larger was the crowd which had filled the streets during the July demonstrations compared with the sparse pickets around the Winter Palace on the day the Provisional Government was overthrown, the 25th October (7th November New Style).

What Lenin's adversaries in the Central Committee would not assess at its real value was the incapacity of the Provisional Government to organise its own defence. Kerensky relied on the support of the Cossacks of the Petrograd garrison but for no good reason: he had over the past few days ruffled their feelings by forbidding them to march in a large religious procession for fear it would degenerate into a counter-revolutionary demonstration. Lenin's political instinct told him that the Provisional Government would not put up any resistance. Trotsky and his close subordinate Antonov-Ovseenko were in full control of the Red Guards among the Petrograd factory-workers and could also rely on the support of the Kronstadt garrison. These forces, Lenin was advised, would follow the instructions of the Central Committee of the Bolshevik party without awaiting confirmation from the Soviet. He was not unaware, moreover, that the Bolsheviks would have only a small majority at the Second Congress of Soviets and would have to fight desperately for a resolution calling for an overthrow of Kerensky's cabinet. This, and his knowledge of Kerensky's weakness, prompted Lenin to insist on the seizure of power without further delay.

On the night of 25th-26th October Red Guards occupied strategic points in the city and Kerensky, realising that he had no grip on the Petrograd garrison to oppose the Bolsheviks, left the capital in search of help from the front. The Provisional Government was in permanent session in the ex-Tsar's Winter Palace, where they were defended by a handful of officer cadets and the Women's Battalion. The Palace was infiltrated by a back door and the Government was arrested and incarcerated in the Peter-Paul Fortress.

Despite the fact that Lenin's policy bears the mark of acute political judgment and ability, we should remember that it was not until the news of the arrest of the Provisional Government was confirmed and announced at the Second Congress of Soviets that Lenin again appeared in public, without the fuzzy wig which had helped transform his bald head into that of the unknown soldier K. Ivanov.

The seizure of power was proclaimed in special issues of

Left: Checking passes outside the Smolny Institute, an exclusive girls' school which became the Bolshevik party headquarters

87

the daily papers throughout Russia, but there was no guarantee that the orders and decrees of the new government would be regarded as having legal force in Moscow or in any of the other provincial centres of Russia. Nor was there any indication that the troops at the front or the High Command in Mogilev would submit to the People's Commissars, that is, the Bolshevik Government. The SRs who had managed to win the sympathies of the Russian peasantry and to obtain an absolute majority in the elections to the Constituent Assembly, which took place only a fortnight after the seizure of power, considered the Bolshevik Government as usurpers and refused to co-operate. True, a relatively small splinter group of the SR party including the hysterical Maria Spiridonova negotiated for entry into the Bolshevik Government, that is, into both the Council of Commissars and the Central Executive Committee of the Congress of Soviets. And even Mensheviks seemed ready to negotiate with the new men in power, whom they had known all their lives as political opponents in the cosmopolitan cafes of so many Western European capitals, provided their freedom of political action was assured.

Lenin did not dare to reject these tentative approaches out of hand, particularly as rumours were reaching him that Kerensky was moving with strong forces from the front to crush the Bolsheviks in Petrograd, and fighting continued in Moscow. Lenin therefore agreed that Kamenev should negotiate with the other parties which were strongly entrenched in the all-important trade-union organisation of the Russian railways, known as Vikzhel. It has never been made absolutely clear who in these negotiations was cheating whom. It seems, however, that Kamenev really believed at the beginning of the negotiations that a mixed socialist government was possible. On the other hand there is clear evidence that Lenin never took these negotiations seriously and let them drag on in order to avert the formation of an anti-communist coalition on a large scale. He broke off these negotiations only after Kerensky's detachment was put to flight and the seven-day battle in Moscow terminated by the surrender of the anti-communist forces.

Contact with other provincial centres was erratic. The seizure of local power by the soviets was carried out in whatever way local conditions permitted and beyond the ken of the central government (if we accept this term when referring to the Bolshevik leadership of those days). In Petrograd during the first two weeks after the arrest of the Provisional Government a kind of ghost cabinet,

Top right: Revolutionary sailors from Kronstadt, the Baltic fortress near Petrograd. Bottom: Red Guards outside Smolny

presided over by the right-wing socialist economist, Professor Prokopovich, maintained a shadowy existence and even had its money orders honoured by the State Bank. Contrary to what had happened in the February Revolution, the middle and lower ranks in the ministries taken over by the People's Commissars stopped turning up for work. The situation in the armed forces was even more confusing. On the whole, the Soldiers' Committees of the various units were dominated by strong supporters of the Provisional Government and refused to take orders from the Council of the People's Commissars. Kerensky had vanished into thin air, and General Dukhonin, who was left in charge of the GHQ, refused to enter into armistice talks with the Germans and Austrians, nor would he permit his subordinates to do so.

But Lenin did not lose his bearings for a minute. He called as many Bolsheviks from Kronstadt as was necessary to protect the main services, and he despatched Ensign Krylenko as Commander-in-Chief of the Russian armed forces, to headquarters to take over from Dukhonin. The old general felt in duty bound to meet Krylenko's train and to hand over the reins of power to him. Their meeting was formal but not unfriendly. However, as soon as Dukhonin descended from the railway carriage he was killed by Krylenko's bodyguards. He had the consolation of a full-scale military funeral a few days later.

The officers at the front, who refused to take orders from the new government, simply deserted their posts and the soldiers elected their own replacements to carry on the day-to-day business of their units. Even so, it took a certain time for the enormous body of the army to decompose in the atmosphere of despair, cowardice, *sauve qui peut,* inhumanity, and sheer criminality.

At first the belief was widespread in Russia that the Bolsheviks would not be able to cope with affairs of state and would soon have to be replaced by more reasonable men. The Bolsheviks themselves maintained their optimism by remaining faithful to the idea of world revolution which would put an end to the war and capitalist domination. But among the more moderate Bolsheviks at the very top of the hierarchy strong feelings against Lenin's tactics built up around Kamenev and Zinoviev, who had opposed the armed rising. They saw that the negotiations with the other socialist parties would lead to nothing and were a deceptive manoeuvre by Lenin, and they therefore decided to resign from the Council of the People's Commissars in protest against the establishment of a regime which would have to depend for its security on the widespread use of political terror. They quickly realised, however, that as long as Lenin remained in power there would be no scope for them to pursue their aims,

that outside the party no political force would be tolerated, and they soon crept penitently back to the fold.

Lenin did not take these defections seriously: they were a hangover of bourgeois democratic prejudices which affected even tested revolutionaries. He had greater apprehensions about the morale of the rank and file of his supporters. Atrocities were being committed every day on an enormous scale all over Russia. One took place in Petrograd in a hospital in which two very sick men, ex-ministers of the Provisional Government, the Kadets Kokoshkin and Shingarev, were killed in cold blood by a gang of Kronstadt sailors. When such atrocities were reported to Lenin he would delegate his trusted friend Bonch-Bruevich to investigate the case. Bonch-Bruevich's brief account of his experience with the Kronstadt gang, who had been carried to the extreme of cruelty by cocaine-intoxicated agitators, is entitled *Horrific Aspects of the Revolution*. Horrific or not, Bonch-Bruevich, like the gang itself, accepted such brutality as an inevitable feature of the great historic moment.

Left: Russia's new rulers. **Left-hand column from top:** *Madame Kollontay, later ambassador to Mexico and Sweden; Kamenev; Zinoviev; Radek.* **Right-hand column:** *Molotov, who remained a Party leader till 1957; Bukharin; Sverdlov, President of the Central Executive Committee of the Soviets, who died in 1919; Dzerzhinsky, fanatical head of the Soviet security police*

Chapter 6
Consolidation of the Soviet Regime

In two respects the first few weeks of Lenin's political domination in Russia were marked by what could be, with reservation, considered successes. First of all, he managed to enter into direct peace negotiations with the German government. A deputation headed by Admiral Count Keyserling and Count Mirbach arrived in Petrograd for preliminary negotiations concerning the exchange of prisoners. After the conclusion of the armistice, on 15th December, peace negotiations were to be started in earnest between the makeshift government of the Bolsheviks and the Imperial Government of Germany. Weak attempts by some German Social Democrats, including the notorious Parvus, to secure the participation of socialist deputies from the Reichstag in a neutral capital such as Stockholm were turned down by Lenin and never had a chance of success at the Wilhelmstrasse.

Lenin's second political success was the entry into the Soviet Government of another party, the Left SRs led by Spiridonova and Kamkov. He welcomed this development particularly in view of the forthcoming Constituent Assembly which was scheduled at last to meet on 18th January (New Style).

But neither the peace negotiations nor the participation of the Left SRs turned out as Lenin had hoped. Another step taken by Lenin in those days has however left a profound mark both on the period when he was the ruler of Russia and on our own times. Immediately after the seizure of power a number of virtually self-appointed bodies made it their business to arrest people whom they considered a danger to the regime or with whom they wished to settle scores. The most notable of such bodies was headed by Felix Dzerzhinsky, a fanatical revolutionary who had, like many other revolutionaries, suffered severe treatment in Tsarist prisons. On about 20th December the Extraordinary Commission for the Struggle against Black-marketeering, Sabotage, and Counter-revolution was formed. It was of short duration but went

Left: Trotsky, instructed by Lenin to buy time at any price, sets off for the Brest-Litovsk peace talks with Germany

down in history under the name of Cheka (formed from the Russian initials for Extraordinary Commission). It has been replaced by numerous other government organs of various titles, but the primary function of state terror has remained their permanent task.

At first the central and local Chekas, not always officially subordinate to each other, carried out arrests and shot delinquents without trial and after a brief investigation, even though the law which had abolished the death penalty was still in force. Later, when they were centralised through Moscow, the Chekas formally became investigatory organs for political and economic crimes, and their decisions came before the Military Revolutionary Tribunal formed in the course of the Civil War. In practice, however, the Military Revolutionary Tribunal did not interfere with the decisions of the Cheka but merely rubber-stamped them. In the turbulent years following the Bolshevik seizure of power an organisation with its own information service and with the power of life or death over any citizen acquired in the eyes of the population paramount importance. It was to this institution that Lenin entrusted the task of organising the 'Red Terror', that is, the liquidation of the former ruling class, including the shooting of hostages for acts of terrorism committed against members and employees of the Soviet government.

The nature of Lenin's major acts in the first two months of his rule reveal, as they did then, the instability of his political conduct. In the case of the Brest-Litovsk peace talks Lenin preferred to conduct them as between one sovereign power and another, without participation of the socialist parties as such on either side. It was this that led to the tough German terms in later negotiations. Even the German Embassy Counsellor K.Riezler, who had been a party to the financial machinations in support of the Bolsheviks and who was well informed on their present situation, admitted that such terms could not have been imposed on a Russian government of any other party than the Bolsheviks.

Did Lenin foresee the hard line the Germans and their allies would pursue at Brest-Litovsk? He certainly nourished the hope that internal unrest and social revolution would break out at any moment in Germany. At the time of the most important political victory in his life, one might say the summit of his influence on the course of world history, Lenin saw himself making only the first step towards his real goal, namely, the great Communist revolution in all capitalist countries, and it is as such that

Right: The civil war. The Illustrated London News *features British tanks sent to help the White general Denikin, 1919*

WHEN THE
GENERAL M

INSPECTING THE
AMBASSADOR

WITH THE BADGE
" UNITED RUSSIA

The situation in Russia is so
that it is not possible to sav

CAPTURED SOME WHILE AGO:
TAKING THE SALUTE AT KIEFF.

MOST VALUABLE IN PURSUING THE BOLSHEVISTS:
A TROOP OF COSSACKS.

KS: THE EMIR OF BOKHARA'S
A RUSSIAN TANK OFFICER.

ARMY, AND THE INSCRIPTION,
URED TRAIN USED AT KIEIF

INSPECTING THE BRITISH-TRAINED RUSSIAN TANK CORPS:
GENERAL DENIKIN.

news from there, on the whole, so unreliable,   forces.——The "chevron" on the armoured train is the red, white, and blue badge of

he regarded the revolutionary changes which occurred in Russia. Without the world revolution the Russian episode appeared to him potentially as much of a dead end as the Paris Commune had been. To ensure that this did not happen he must hold onto power in Russia even if it involved a degree of unsocialist policy and behaviour. In the event the Germans imposed a treaty of unprecedented severity: the dismemberment of Soviet territory, the formation of a large buffer-state, an independent Ukraine in the south, an indemnity paid under a treaty which was to remain secret and was signed only in August 1918, all of which conditions were designed to make Russia into a vassal-state of Imperial Germany.

While recognising the monstrosity of complying with the German demands, Lenin insisted that they should be accepted without delay and he rejected as infantile and unrealistic all appeals for a revolutionary crusade by the proletariat. A large group of the most prominent Bolsheviks including Bukharin, Kollontay, Radek, and others, split from the main body of the party in order to create a movement of Left Communists opposed to Brest-Litovsk. This tension was of fundamental importance up to August 1918 and might have cost Lenin his leadership of the party if the collapse of the German Front in the west on 8th August and the rout that followed had not taken Germany out of the war and made the Brest-Litovsk *diktat,* in the words of its historian Wheeler-Bennett, a 'forgotten treaty'.

What this tension achieved, however, was at first the partial and later the mass elimination of the SRs from the Soviet apparatus. They were strongly represented at the Third and later at the Fifth Congress of Soviets and would certainly have had an overwhelming majority had not the principle been applied that a vote by an urban worker at elections to the All-Russian Council of the Soviets was equal to the votes of five peasants. They left the government at the time of Brest-Litovsk but they continued their work in the soviets and in the Central Executive Committee of the Soviets, and they occupied important positions in particular in the Cheka. The thunderbolt of Lenin's annihilating fury struck them only on 6th June 1918, which is noted in Soviet history books and elsewhere as the day of the assassination of Count Mirbach by the Left SRs and of their rising against the Soviet government. Some people, both among Lenin's entourage and among those who have studied his behaviour, have strongly suspected that it was he who instigated the assassination of the German envoy by a member of the Left SR party and that the government's

Right: Recruiting poster calls on workers to serve the Red Flag

measures against the Left SRs in reply to the assassination were a provocation by Lenin designed to make them rise and thus be more easily eliminated altogether. Perhaps the most damning evidence of Lenin's responsibility for this affair is that the main assassin, Blyumkin, was not sentenced and was reinstated in the Soviet secret service.

In a sense, it was the passive resistance of a part of the Central Committee to the seizure of power on 25th October that had facilitated Lenin's return to the helm of the party during the Second Congress of Soviets. It is remarkable with what self-confidence he played the role of victor in a battle which he had by no means yet won. Knowing that he could not offer the bread which had been promised in the slogan 'Peace, Land, and Bread!' Lenin concentrated all his demagogy on claiming the merit of establishing immediate peace and of allowing the peasants to seize the land without further ceremony. He had promised that 'a just and immediate peace will everywhere find an ardent response among the international proletarian masses', and to guarantee this ardour Lenin announced that he would publish all the secret agreements made by the Tsarist government and the Allies during the war, thus disclosing the 'predatory character of the capitalist slaughterhouse'. But the ardent response was not forthcoming and instead of a democratic peace Russia was offered the most degrading, 'obscene' as Lenin put it, peace conditions by the Central Powers.

When the Left Communists and the Left SRs called for a revolutionary war against the German domination of the borderlands Lenin replied, forgetting his wartime championship of self-determination, that the Soviet government had no right to jeopardise the existence of a socialist order in Russia by waging such a war merely because the right of self-determination was being denied a number of nations (Poland, Lithuania, Courland, and so on). No Marxist, he said, could oppose this thesis without breaking with the very foundations of Marxism.

But as a political contortionist Lenin demonstrated his supreme skill in his handling of the Constituent Assembly and the closely connected problem, in such a predominantly agricultural country, of agrarian reform. On 26th October 1917 at the Second Congress of Soviets he announced the land policy of his government, in which he accepted the principles worked out by the All-Russian Congress of Peasant Soviets, where the SRs were in a

Right: Leather shortages forced the Red Army to fight in bark shoes, 1920. Far right: The Bolshevik view of big business and the·Church weeping over the graves of the White generals contrasts with an extreme White Guard lampoon of Trotsky

Foreign intervention, 1918-19

Principal forces opposing Bolshevik armies

1 Americans	**9** Letts
2 Baltic Germans	**10** Lithuanians
3 British	**11** Poles
4 Cossacks	**12** Rumanians
5 Czechs	**13** White Russians
6 Finns	**14** Serbs
7 French	**15** Ukrainians
8 Italians	

Furthest advance
of anti-Bolshevik
forces 1918-19

Under Bolshevik
control Nov.1918

Established
Russian frontiers
Mar.1921-Oct.1939

Arctic Ocean

SWEDEN

Murmansk

3 **14**

Kem

6

FINLAND

6

Onega

Archangel

8
1
3

Kronstadt

Baltic
Sea

Petrograd

Vologda

Volga R.

Perm

13
9

Riga

Tver

Nizhni-
Novgorod

Ufa

5

2
10

Vitebsk

Moscow

Kazan

POLAND

Warsaw

Minsk

Tula

Simbirsk

Samara

Orenburg

13

Gomel

Orel

Tambov

Don R.

11

13

Kursk

Kiev

Kharkov

12
7

Dnieper R.

15
4
13

Guriev

Odessa

Rostov

Astrakhan

RUMANIA
BULGARIA

Kherson
Sevastopol

Black Sea

Caspian
Sea

Constantinople

Batum

3

3

Tiflis

Baku

Kars

TURKEY

Erivan

majority. Answering some dissatisfied mutterings from the ranks of his own party, Lenin said: 'And even if the peasants continue to follow the Socialist Revolutionaries and even if they give the Socialist Revolutionaries a majority in the Constituent Assembly we shall say "so be it".' Life itself, he said, will bring the peasants' point of view closer to the Bolshevik programme. And at the peak of demogogical hypocrisy, Lenin claimed: 'Russia is great and local conditions differ from place to place; we believe that the peasantry will itself, better than we can, find a correct solution to this question.'

In the elections to the Constituent Assembly which were carried out under a system devised by the Provisional Government, the Bolsheviks fought an energetic campaign and gained about one quarter of the seats. Those among them who were elected to the Constituent Assembly started working out the position the party would take in the Assembly even before it convened. These activities of the Bolshevik group of the Constituent Assembly caused considerable worry both to Lenin and to his Central Committee, since many provincial party members were not schooled in the subtleties of Marxist dialectics and continued to regard the Constituent Assembly as the organ through which the common will of the people was to find its clearest expression. But Lenin was quick to react to this threat. At a special meeting of the Central Committee he proposed that the present group be dismissed and a new one put in its place, one that would take greater account of the 'real conditions of class struggle and civil war'.

This was, of course, more of a threat than a decision. In eighteen theses Lenin laid down the Bolshevik attitude to the Constituent Assembly, and in the last of these we find the nub of his position: the only way to solve the crisis arising from a conflict between the election results and the will of the people, i.e. a non-Bolshevik majority, is to recall certain deputies and to replace them with others, a procedure to which the Assembly must agree. The Assembly must further recognise the Soviet Government, the Revolution, Soviet policy on peace, land, and workers' control, and finally, must decisively join the struggle against the White counter-revolution.

Lenin himself attended the meeting of the Constituent Assembly on 18th January 1918 having first ordered the military suppression of all street demonstrations. He lounged somnolently yawning and grinning at the flow of oratory from Chernov, the leader of the SRs, and Tseretelli, the leader of the Mensheviks. He ordered the Bolshevik Group to leave the meeting demonstratively as

Left: *Map showing the extent of intervention in Western Russia*

soon as the Constituent Assembly refused to recognise the decrees of the Central Executive Committee of the Soviet and the Council of People's Commissars. He gave detailed instructions to the armed guards he had placed all around the chamber not to point their rifles at the speakers or other members of the Assembly, nor to use brute force on them, but just to let them disperse and then prevent them from re-entering the building. The Constituent Assembly, in which millions of Russians had placed their last hope that a change for the better might be made in the course of this, to them, totally bewildering revolution – this body was cynically dismissed by Lenin.

How did Lenin himself view the day in which the Bolshevik party (soon to be renamed as Communist) so effortlessly swept away the political representation of the whole nation? 'I have wasted a day, my friends,' having gone to this demonstration of counter-revolutionary aspirations, camouflaged in the socialist phraseology of Chernov and Tseretelli. 'What a heavy, dull, and boring day in the elegant surroundings of the Tauride Palace, which is so different even in appearance from the Smolny Institute [the Bolshevik headquarters], just as elegant but dead bourgeois parliamentarism is so different from the proletarian, simple Soviet apparatus, in many ways still disorderly and unfinished, but nevertheless live and viable. There in the old world of bourgeois parliamentarism, leaders of hostile classes and hostile groups of the bourgeoisie were fencing with each other. Here, in the new world of the proletarian and peasant socialist state, the oppressed classes are doing their work in a coarse and clumsy way . . .'

This fragment which was published two years after his death remained unfinished. But its unspoken message is clear enough. Lenin evidently believed that once he had skilfully and in a single moment overthrown all authority, order, and tradition in Russia, his task would be taken over by the wonderful Russian proletariat and the poorest peasantry, and that it would be carried on until the spark which he had ignited in backward Russia spread to a general conflagration in the whole capitalist world, from the ashes of which the Communist phoenix would rise.

As it happened, the people who came and helped to perpetuate the life of Lenin's government were not the workers and poor peasants, but the German Occupation Army which moved deep into Southern Russia and re-

Top left: *Lenin shortly after Dora Kaplan's assassination attempt in 1918, with his old friend Bonch-Bruevich.* **Top right:** *Lenin in Red Square, Moscow, May Day 1919.* **Bottom:** *The orator, 1920. Later Soviet prints eradicated Trotsky (right)*

mained poised for a final leap at the gates of Petrograd. Considerable sums were allotted by the German exchequer for the maintenance of the Soviet government in power. By June however the German envoy and his grey eminence Dr Riezler started pressing on their government the need to get rid of the impossible Bolsheviks and to replace them by another puppet government of moderate right-wing constitutionalists, to whom, of course, certain concessions would have to be made.

It was at this time that, most conveniently for Lenin, the Left SRs assassinated the German envoy and were lured into a kind of civil war with the troops of the Council of People's Commissars which ended in the crushing of the mutiny and the extinction of the Left SR party in a matter of hours. A week later Lenin's government took a decision which might have been precautionary but looked rather like a panicky act of personal vengeance. They allowed the local soviet in Ekaterinburg, in the Urals, to murder Nicholas II, his wife, children, doctor, and personal servants. How little faith the Soviet government had in its own ability to act in accordance with the wishes of the people may be judged from the fact that in spite of the detailed information available, they issued a purposely false communiqué announcing the execution of the ex-Tsar but reassuring the people that his son and wife had been taken to a place of safety. These executions as well as the killing of other members of the Imperial family were, however, helpful to Lenin's regime insofar as they made a counter-revolutionary monarchist movement virtually impossible to organise.

Far more important for the stabilisation of the Soviet regime was the defeat of Germany by the Entente. This relieved Lenin of the fear of German intervention and made it possible for him to declare the Brest-Litovsk treaty null and void. There remained however the threat of a civil war by all sorts of non-Bolshevik elements in the remote parts of the country operating with the help of the badly organised and parsimonious support of the former Western Allies. The real effect of the civil war in Russia was, however, to force the Soviet government to recreate a fighting army which could only be done by first abolishing the principle of indiscipline that had dismembered the old army. This reform was carried out ruthlessly and systematically by that genius of improvisation, Trotsky.

As for the intervention by the Entente, it petered out because it had been conceived mainly as a means of re-

Top right: White émigré cartoon depicts the sacrifice of Russia on the altar of the International. Lenin directs, Trotsky stabs, Kerensky watches. *Bottom:* Lenin opens the 3rd International

opening the Eastern Front against Germany, and thus to continue supplying the White armies came to appear as an ill-advised and unjustified intervention in Russian internal affairs. If anything, the civil war helped the Bolshevik regime in many respects: it above all justified the organisation of a ruthless and generally efficient wartime administration; it marshalled the sympathies of large masses of peasants who had seized the landowners' estates and were easily convinced that with the fall of the Soviet government they would have to surrender them back to their 'rightful owners'. In addition, the political unrest in Central Europe, involving the formation of new independent states and the collapse of Imperial Germany and Austro-Hungary, raised Lenin's hopes for world revolution and contributed considerably to Bolshevik morale.

In reality there was little ground for optimism. The fighting capacity of the Red Army was tested in the war with the even younger and less well-endowed small state of Poland and it proved wanting. The Russian peasantry united against the arbitrary and brutal expropriation of their produce by the Soviet authorities. The towns were depopulated and the very thin stratum of industrial workers in Russia completely disappeared owing partly to the flight of workers into the villages where they might find food, partly by recruitment into the Red Army where many died in the fighting or in a terrible typhus epidemic, and partly by absorption into the ever-growing bureaucratic apparatus of the Bolshevik state.

Lenin had no scruples about using terrorist methods of repression against the representatives of the very class in whose name he acted as dictator. On 9th July 1919, after a number of typographers and railway men had been shot by the Cheka, Lenin wrote: 'Our business is to put the question straightforwardly. What is better? To pick out and put into prison, sometimes even to shoot hundreds of traitors from the ranks of the Kadets, non-party people, Mensheviks, and Socialist Revolutionaries who come out — some of them with arms, others with conspiracies, others again, as typographers and railway men belonging to the Mensheviks, with agitation against mobilisation and the like — who come out against the Soviet power, that is, in favour of [the White General] Denikin? Or should we let things go so far as to permit Kolchak and Denikin to murder and shoot and flog to death tens of thousands of workers and peasants? The choice between these two alternatives is easy.'

*Top left: White-clad Bolshevik troops move across the ice to Kronstadt, 1921. The sailors of the Baltic fleet, once called by Trotsky 'the pride and glory of the Revolution', demanded a return to the liberties of 1917. **Bottom:** But the Red Army won*

Thus all political problems were reduced to the one essential problem of the survival of Bolshevik power. But the civil war depleted Russia's seemingly inexhaustible resources and brought production almost to a standstill. According to Bolshevik sources, by the winter of 1920/1 the production of crude oil had fallen to one-third, coal to one-sixth, cotton to one-fifth, flax to one-sixth, sugar-beet to one-quarter, and cast iron to one-twentieth of what it had been, not before the war, but in 1916. Thus it came about that at the beginning of 1921, after the conclusion of a peace treaty with Poland and the introduction of Soviet governments totally controlled by Moscow in the Ukraine, Byelorussia, and the Transcaucasian Federation, Lenin began to think of a way to make the wheels of industry turn again and to lure the peasants into producing enough to feed the cities as well as themselves. He produced his privately worked-out scheme for reform in March 1921 at the Tenth Party Congress to the great surprise and shock of many of his closest followers and admirers. Private enterprise was to be allowed on a limited scale, competing where necessary with the state sector in the production of consumer goods. Concessions were to be given to foreign firms for large-scale construction. A fixed tax in kind was to be imposed on the peasantry after the payment of which they would be free to sell any surplus in free markets which would be held in the towns.

These were the proposals for a New Economic Policy (NEP). The moment was both pressing and opportune. While the Congress was meeting in Moscow, extraordinary events were taking place in Petrograd and in the naval base of Kronstadt. The sailors of Kronstadt had never gone through with the reform Trotsky had imposed on the army and they still had Sailors' Committees on battleships and other units of the Baltic Fleet. When the Kronstadt Soviet was about to be re-elected they declared that they would not have the Soviet appointed by the party, but would have it elected in free competition with all socialist parties and the anarchists. Attempts to persuade them otherwise ended in failure and the Kronstadt garrison appealed to the country at large to support its demands for free elections and an end to the Bolshevik monopoly of power.

Lenin's reaction is an example of Leninist cant at its best. To the press and foreign governments he spoke of the Kronstadt mutiny as a White Guardist adventure of minor dimensions, but in his speech to the Tenth Congress he claimed that Kronstadt spelt danger for the

Right: The hammer and sickle, with other symbols of socialism, upheld by the nationalities of the USSR. Soviet painting

Bolshevik government greater than that from Kolchak, Denikin, and Yudenich put together.

He gave his blessing for three hundred members of the Congress to go to the shores of the Baltic to agitate among selected troops who, with unprecedented ferocity, went on to crush the Kronstadt mutiny on 18th March. No sooner had the intrepid 300 left the Congress than Lenin presented the remaining delegates with two resolutions, which were substantively to affect internal relations in the Party and its contacts with the population at large. In his view the majority of the Russian people belonged to an indeterminate class, 'semi-proletarian' or 'semi-bourgeois'. Under certain conditions, as in 1917, these masses would support a government which was genuinely working for a socialist order, i.e. Lenin's. The Kronstadt rising, Lenin lamented, showed how wavering these masses were. They must not be allowed to succumb to anti-Bolshevik propaganda or to produce an ideology based on the property instincts always present in the mind of the semi-proletarian. Therefore, all state and cultural activities must be watched and controlled with extreme stringency by the Communist government itself. Syndicalist plans for producers' councils and congresses could not be tolerated. In particular, no nonparty citizen might take the initiative in organising a meeting or any other political action without the consent and supervision of the party. Lenin concluded this resolution by reaffirming that the destiny of the revolution must not be left to the mood of the majority of the population, which was unstable and corruptible.

His second resolution reasserted the principle of 'democratic centralism', which ruled that once a higher party committee has taken a decision it should not be discussed nor the decision criticised by individual members or lower party organisations. No lobbying or appeal against the decisions of a superior organ of the party could be made by any subordinate organisation. As for the supreme organ of the party, the Central Committee, Lenin's resolution stipulated that its members must carry out and accept without murmur or protest resolutions passed by a majority, and that any attempt to mobilise contrary party opinion should be considered as fractionalism and might be punished by expulsion from the Central Committee. This part of the resolution was to remain secret and not to be published with the minutes of the Congress. It was, however, soon revealed when it was applied to the various types of deviationists: first Trotsky and his friends, and later on the left and right oppositions.

Top right: Paper currency was made worthless by war, famine, and economic stagnation. *Bottom:* The changing economic pattern

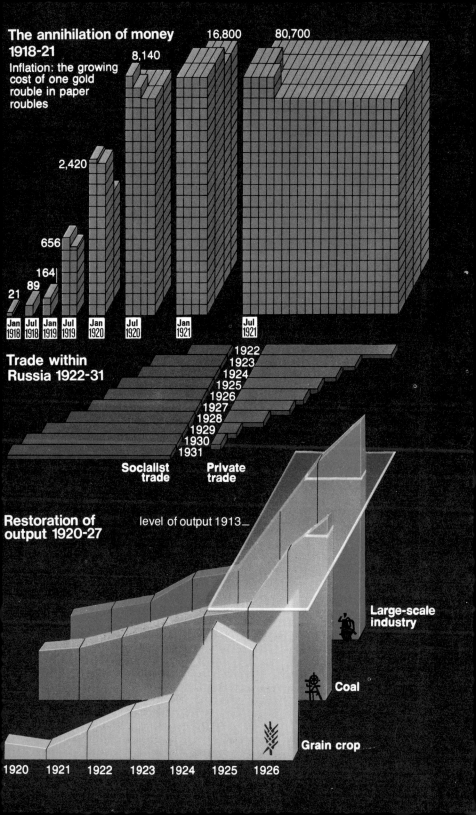

The annihilation of money 1918-21

Inflation: the growing cost of one gold rouble in paper roubles

80,700

16,800

8,140

2,420

656

164

89

21

| Jan 1918 | Jul 1918 | Jan 1919 | Jul 1919 | Jan 1920 | Jul 1920 | Jan 1921 | Jul 1921 |

Trade within Russia 1922-31

1922
1923
1924
1925
1926
1927
1928
1929
1930
1931

Socialist trade   **Private trade**

Restoration of output 1920-27

level of output 1913

Large-scale industry

Coal

Grain crop

1920   1921   1922   1923   1924   1925   1926

Chapter 7
The Last Days of Lenin

In spite of his boisterous character, his considerable physical strength, and his careful attention to contemporary hygiene, Lenin cannot be called a very healthy person. As early as 1895 on his first journey abroad he suffered from some undisclosed ailment, was seen by doctors, and even stayed for a time in a sanatorium in Switzerland. Later on he suffered from headaches and insomnia, possibly a consequence of too much reading in libraries and intellectual overwork in general. In August 1918 he was shot at by Dora Kaplan, a Socialist Revolutionary terrorist, and was hit by two bullets at close range. One of the bullets remained unextracted in his neck. He seemed to recover completely from his wounds and they did not interrupt his work for any length of time.

However, towards the end of 1921, just when the New Economic Policy began to take shape and show some results, the first symptoms of a grave nervous disturbance became noticeable. He had to interrupt his work through exhaustion, dizziness, acute headaches, and tormenting insomnia. He retired to the countryside at Gorki, near Moscow, and continued to bombard the Council of People's Commissars with instructions, orders, and admonitions. He took particular interest in the first Soviet show-trial, that of the Socialist Revolutionaries. In this connection he wrote to the Commissar of Justice, Kursky, who was compiling a Soviet Criminal Code: 'In my opinion it is necessary to extend the death penalty by shooting to all types of conspiratorial activity by Mensheviks, Socialist Revolutionaries, and the like. We must work out a formula which would establish a link between these activities and those of the international bourgeoisie and its struggle against us (bribery of the press and of agents, preparation for war and the like).' The letter remained unpublished until 1937 when it was used to justify the notorious show-trials of Lenin's closest collaborators.

At the end of May 1922, whilst still in Gorki, Lenin

Left: Lenin after his first stroke, in Gorki with his wife, 1922

suffered his first stroke: 'the first bell' as he said, alluding to the railway custom of ringing a bell three times before the train left. The paralysis was not complete and yielded gradually to treatment. Lenin recovered enough in the course of 1922 to be able to follow current events and even make a short appearance at the Eleventh Party Congress.

Three factors determined the activities of the sick man in this last year of his political existence: the fight against his illness and the prohibitions imposed on him on medical grounds; the consolidation of the Soviet Union through incorporation of almost the entire territory of the former Russian Empire; and the question of his succession. As soon as his illness was recognised as a disease of the central nervous system the medical authorities recommended absolute rest, fresh air, and the avoidance of all emotional excitement caused by unwelcome and worrying political information. Lenin himself had always insisted that the party leaders should look upon the maintenance of their health as one of their many political duties and would order absolute rest for comrades who had been overworking. Following his principles the Politburo of the Central Committee insisted on a strict observation of the rules imposed by the doctors and appointed Stalin supervisor of Lenin's sick-room regime.

Lenin fought back, demanding to be informed of what was going on at least through the newspapers. As his condition improved he was visited by members of the government and the Politburo who, whatever their intention, could not leave Lenin's questions unanswered. When he found out that things were being concealed from him he became angry, as Krupskaya reports when she tried to hide from him the death in exile of his old friend-turned-enemy, Julius Martov.

Krupskaya's position was particularly delicate. Her devotion to the dying man was total but she herself was a party member, and political, especially conspiratorial political activity, was for her, as for Lenin himself, the very breath of life. It was because she could not prevent herself from discussing the business of the Central Committee with her husband that she became involved in a conflict with Stalin who, with his usual brutality, became insolent and abusive. The last letter written by Lenin to Stalin was a demand for a complete apology to Krupskaya. Stalin never forgot Krupskaya's behaviour and always showed profound contempt for her after he came to power, even threatening her with the 'revelation' that she was not Lenin's real widow.

Right: Opening of a hydro-power station in 1922. The year before, Lenin announced his dramatic change of direction, the NEP

Упорным трудом, молотом, плугом и лопатой мы построим наше народное хозяйство.

ЭЛЕКТРОФИКАЦИЯ УКРЕПЛЕНИЕ СОВЕТСКОЙ ЛАСТИ ..ТЬ к КОММ...

In the last quarter of 1922 Lenin got his doctor's permission to dictate notes every day for a period of a quarter to half an hour at a time. The result is a series of remarkable statements which were partly concealed from the world and the population of the Soviet Union until the Twentieth Congress in 1956. They disclose the helpless amazement of the founder of the Soviet state at the behaviour of the monster to which he had given life.

A recurrent feature of these notes is the demand for an organisation which would check on the spot how faithfully the instructions of the central authorities were being followed. The office of the 'Workers and Peasants Inspection' which had been created to do this work had become, Lenin complained, an inefficient, bureaucratised machine, but the advice he gave for its reorganisation was rather ineffectual.

The workings of the New Economic Policy and its political implications were another matter of concern for Lenin. The system was accepted by the party leadership not without murmur and grumblings. Yet it worked more or less as expected in the industrial sphere. The situation in the countryside and the reaction of the peasantry were more disappointing. Many in the party leadership feared that the economic freedom given to the peasantry would create a class with property interests and a 'property-owner mentality', and that at some time this class would gain the upper hand in the running of the state. This would spell doom for the idea of a socialist revolution. Lenin countered these fears by claiming that the introduction of modern machinery and in particular electric power to the countryside would lead the peasants to unite in producers' co-operatives, based not on capitalist but on socialist forms of ownership.

A further question which obviously worried Lenin beyond endurance was that of national minorities in the newly formed Federation of Soviet Republics. This question came to a head over the confrontation of the Moscow Bolsheviks with the leadership of the Georgian Communist Party. Lenin wrote on 30th December 1922: 'It seems I have greatly wronged the workers of Russia by not intervening energetically and firmly enough in the infamous question of autonomisation, officially known, I believe, as the question of the Union of the Socialist Soviet Republics.' In this note Lenin condemns the efforts of such people as Stalin, Dzerzhinsky, and Ordzhonikidze to concentrate all administrative power in the bureaucratic apparatus in Moscow, although he agreed that foreign policy, defence, and international trade should be dealt with in centralised offices.

The majority of the Politburo members wanted to go much further and take over the administration of finance

and the railways of the so-called 'Union Republics' and submit the local administrators to the dictate of Moscow. Lenin bitterly commented that in their effort to enforce this policy the 'Great Russian chauvinists', especially those of non-Russian origin, had had 'recourse to very dubious methods, disrupting party organisation of the national minorities, even manhandling local political opponents'.

This letter was a good example of Lenin's fulminating polemical style and it is amazing that he could still write in this manner at a time when his brain must have been functioning in a most abnormal way. It is plain from these notes that Lenin was not satisfied with what he saw being done with the fruits of his five-year labour in building the Soviet empire. Yet he never doubted the principle on which this empire was to be built. He argued on the one hand in favour of administrative decentralisation, but on the other he pointed out that this implied no political danger as long as the party remained totally centralised.

The struggle for succession

But Lenin's chief preoccupation was the question as to who would succeed him. The document he dictated on this question is known as 'Lenin's Testament'. Clearly Lenin did not nominate a successor, nor did he want to. Instead he gave character assessments of a number of his under-lings, always pointing out that they were lacking some essential quality for leadership. But one thing Lenin made absolutely clear in the text and in the appendix to the 'testament', and this was that Stalin was not to be his successor and that he should be removed from the position of enormous power which he had contrived to accumulate. Rude and uncultured, a cook who could prepare only peppery dishes, Stalin appears odious in Lenin's 'testament'.

At the beginning of 1923 Lenin thought of taking action himself to unseat Stalin from his position and sought people within the Communist leadership on whom he could rely to carry out this operation. The scene, as he saw it, was to be the Twelfth Party Congress at which Lenin intended to 'throw his bomb'. But he started preparing for the Congress as early as March 1923, relying on the support of Kamenev and Trotsky. The Congress was to take place in Moscow on 17th April. On 6th March Lenin, knowing what was going on from the Central Committee files on the Georgian 'affair', sent a telegram to the Georgian Bolsheviks as follows: 'To Comrades Mdivani, Makharadze, and others. Copies to Comrades

Left: Famine, 1922. American Relief, organised by Herbert Hoover, saved millions from starvation. Three million died

Trotsky and Kamenev. Dear Comrades! With all my heart I am following the development of your affair. I am outraged by the gross behaviour of Ordzhonikidze and by the encouragement he got from Stalin and Dzerzhinsky. I am preparing notes and a speech for you. With respect. Lenin.' These were the last words Lenin ever dictated. The same day, 6th March, the state of his health deteriorated, a paralysis set in on 10th March, and he lost his speech on the 14th.

Lenin had been mistaken in supposing that he could rely on Kamenev. Quite obviously the plan to succeed Lenin by the triumvirate of Kamenev, Zinoviev, and Stalin to the exclusion of Trotsky was already in the making. Therefore the first thing Kamenev did was to communicate Lenin's note to Stalin.

Stalin must have been greatly reassured by the news of the progressive deterioration in Lenin's health. Thus ended the last attempt of the great revolutionary leader to repair a situation in which he himself had, according to his own words, 'greatly wronged the workers of Russia'.

After the middle of March 1923 Lenin never recovered his speech although he was for a time mobile and seems to have enjoyed sleigh-rides on the snow-covered roads of the manor house near Moscow where he lived under the care of Krupskaya and his sister Maria. Whether he managed even at that time to express any opinions on the political situation, which was for him the result of his life's work, we shall not know as long as the documents of the period and the notes of his nurses and secretaries are in the keeping of the Central Committee of the Party.

That he died a natural death from the destruction of half his brain is attested by the postmortem which non-Russian doctors signed together with their Soviet colleagues. The findings of the medical authorities confirm those of the painter George Annenkov. When he visited the Lenin Institute a few weeks after Lenin's death to study the photographs from which he was commissioned to paint a monumental portrait, he saw there a glass jar in which Lenin's brain was suspended in fluid. One of the hemispheres was sound, full-weight, and clearly showed the convolutions of the brain substance. The other hemisphere, attached to the first by something like a band, was withered, crushed, and not larger than a walnut. 'In a few days,' Annenkov goes on, 'this terrifying jar disappeared from the Institute, I believe for ever. I was told in the Kremlin that it was removed at the request of Krupskaya, which is more than understandable. I heard, however, years later, that it was transferred

Right: Socialist Revolutionaries on trial in 1922. The Cheka's mass terror and growing immunity alarmed many Bolsheviks

118

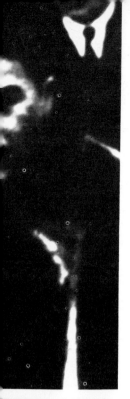

for medical investigation somewhere to Berlin.' In fact, Lenin's brain remained in Russia, there to be dissected minutely by German specialists whose findings were inconclusive.

The question which forces itself upon us is: How long before the physical symptoms of the disease became obvious was Lenin's mentality affected by the gradual destruction of his brain? Was he in full possession of his mental powers at the Tenth Congress in 1921, or during the Civil War, or even at the moment of the seizure of power in 1917? He was certainly a man of extraordinary abilities, immense will-power and perseverance in the pursuit of the aims which he had set himself. But the aims were always so far beyond the possibility of their realisation that most of his life Lenin spent in constricting the circle of his admirers and supporters to the few who would swallow his dreams as a blueprint for the future.

By 1914 he was severely compromised in the eyes of the international socialist movement and surrounded by Tsarist police spies, whom he refused to recognise as such in spite of frequently substantiated exposures. In 1917 it was the initiative of the German government which opened up opportunities for which he could never have hoped but which he knew well how to use. The fact that he had dared to seize power at a moment when his followers were ready to compromise, tergiversate, and settle for the role of opposition in a democratic state, led him to believe that it was his understanding of the dialectics of history that had made possible the incredible achievement of becoming the master of Russia.

Soon he began to realise that this enormous and backward country was hardly the most favourable place in which to inaugurate the dawn of the World Socialist Revolution. Horrified by the crudity and inefficiency of a mushrooming bureaucracy, improvised in the years of the Civil War, he flinched from imposing the force of this instrument on the borderlands, perhaps hoping that, for example in Georgia, a better means for carrying out the first socialist experiment might be found. In this attempt he failed. Betrayed by the men in whom he had put his faith, he let the instrument of his power slip into the hands of the wrong Georgian, Stalin, whom he detested. And Stalin knew how to use it to extremes to which Lenin did not stoop, even at the time of his declining intelligence and consciousness.

Left: The death of Lenin. Top: Stalin as pall-bearer, Mikoyan and Molotov behind. Bottom: The funeral procession, Moscow

Chronology of Events

Note: *The Western Calendar was adopted by the Soviet government in January 1918 in place of the Julian Calendar (used in this book). Thus the October Revolution took place on 25th/26th October old-style, 6th/7th November new-style.*

1870 **10th April**: birth of Vladimir Ilyich Ulyanov (Lenin)

1887 Vladimir becomes a student at Kazan University. His brother Alexander executed for plotting to kill the Tsar (May)

1897 Banishment for three years to Siberia

1898 Formation of the (Marxist) Social Democratic Party in Russia

1900 Except for brief period 1905-7, Lenin (the pseudonym
-17 he adopted in 1901) lives in Western Europe

1903 At its Second Congress, held in London, the Social Democratic party splits into Bolsheviks and Mensheviks

1905 'Bloody Sunday' and country-wide unrest force the Tsar to make concessions, which herald a period of political apathy

1914 **July**: Germany declares war on Russia

1916 **September-October**: strikes gather momentum

1917 The February Revolution. The Petrograd Soviet of Workers' and Soldiers' Deputies is formed; Provisional Government headed by Prince Lvov is set up after Tsar Nicholas II abdicates
February-October: rule of the Provisional Government
April: Lenin and other Bolshevik émigrés return to Petrograd
June: failure of Russian offensive
3rd/4th July: Bolsheviks prematurely organise armed demonstration in Petrograd. Trotsky arrested. Lenin flees to Finland, Kerensky becomes head of government

August: Kornilov affair
September: Bolshevik majorities in Moscow and Petrograd Soviets
10th October: Bolshevik Central Committee resolves that the time is ripe for an armed uprising
25th/26th October: arrest of the Provisional Government in the Winter Palace. Kerensky fails to rally resistance
26th October: Lenin announces victory of the socialist revolution. The new government assumes the name 'Council of People's Commissars'
December: formation of the Cheka (security police). Peace negotiations started with Germany

1918 **January**: Constituent Assembly (420 Socialist Revolutionaries, 225 Bolsheviks) dispersed by Red troops
16th July: murder of Nicholas II, the Tsarina and children at Ekaterinburg

1918 The Civil War. Red Army under Trotsky—after initial
-20 reverses—gradually regains control of Russia from the loose-knit White and Allied forces

1919 **2nd March**: foundation of the Third International (Comintern)

1921 **March**: suppression of the Kronstadt rising in the Baltic Fleet
March: Lenin's New Economic Policy is launched
April: drought brings start of the Great Famine (1921-2)

1922 **26th May**: Lenin's first stroke
November: Lenin ceases regular work

1924 **21st January**: Lenin dies
1st February: Great Britain recognises the Soviet Union

*Top: A baker tramples on an old shop-sign, 'By appointment to the Tsar', 1917 (left); General Kornilov, son of a Cossack village clerk who became C-in-C in July 1917, later killed in action against the Red Army (centre); 'Long Live the Third Communist International!' (right). **Middle**: Red cartoon of White general Kolchak (left); British troops in Vladivostok 1919 (centre); first issue of the Communist International journal, 1st May 1919 (right). **Bottom**: Stalin, Zinoviev, and Kamenev fight to keep out Trotsky after Lenin's death (left); Kalinin, head of state at Lenin's death (centre)*

LONG LIVE THE THIRD COMMUNIST INTERNATIONAL! VIVE LA TROISIÈME INTERNATIONALE COMMUNISTE! EVVIVA IL TERZA INTERNAZIONALE COMMUNISTA! ES LEBE DIE DRITTE KOMMUNISTISCHE INTERNATIONALE!

PROLETARIER ALLER LÄNDER VEREINIGT EUCH!

DIE KOMMUNISTISCHE INTERNATIONALE

№ 1   MOSKAU KREML.   ◆   PETROGRAD SMOLNY.   1 MAI 1919.

Index of main people, places, and events

Authors' suggestions for further reading

Balabanov, Angelica
Impressions of Lenin
University of Michigan 1964
Fischer, Louis
The Life of Lenin
London 1965
Futrell, Michael
Northern Underground
London 1963
Katkov, George
Russia 1917: The February Revolution
London 1967
Payne, Robert
The Life and Death of Lenin
London 1964
Schapiro, Leonard
The Communist Party of the Soviet Union
London 1966
Schapiro, L. and **Reddaway,** P.
(Eds.) *Lenin: The Man, The Theorist, The Leader*
London 1967
Shub, David
Lenin: A Biography
London 1966
Shukman, Harold
Lenin and the Russian Revolution
London 1966
Valentinov, Nicholas
Meetings with Lenin
New York 1953

Library of the 20th Century will include the following titles:

Russia in Revolt
David Floyd
The Second Reich
Harold Kurtz
The Anarchists
Roderick Kedward
Suffragettes International
Trevor Lloyd
War by Time-Table
A.J.P.Taylor
Death of a Generation
Alistair Horne
Suicide of the Empires
Alan Clark
Twilight of the Habsburgs
Z.A.B.Zeman
Early Aviation
Sir Robert Saundby
Birth of the Movies
D.J.Wenden
America Comes of Age
A.E.Campbell
Lenin's Path to Power
G.Katkov and H.Shukman
The Weimar Republic
Sefton Delmer
Out of the Lion's Paw
Constantine Fitzgibbon
Japan: The Years of Triumph
Louis Allen
Communism Takes China
C.P.FitzGerald
Black and White in South Africa
G.H.Le May
Woodrow Wilson
E.A.Ions
France 1918-34
J.P.T.Bury
France 1934-40
W.Knapp
Mussolini's Italy
E.M.Robertson
The Little Dictators
A.Polonsky
Viva Zapata
L.Bethell
The World Depression
Malcolm Falkus
Stalin's Russia
A.Nove
The Brutal Reich
Donald Watt
The Spanish Civil War
Raymond Carr
Munich: Czech Tragedy
K.G.Robbins

George Katkov emigrated with his family from Russia in 1921 and settled in Prague where he studied Philosophy and Indian languages and literature. In 1939 he came to Oxford where he continued his studies into contemporary Russian history. He is at present a Fellow of St Antony's College, Oxford, and Lecturer in Soviet Institutions at Oxford University. He has written several articles on contemporary Russian history and a book, *Russia 1917: The February Revolution.* He is now working on a History of the Provisional Government in Russia in 1917.

Harold Shukman has carried out research into Russian history at St Antony's College, Oxford, and at Harvard and Stanford Universities, USA. He is at present Lecturer in Modern Russian History at Oxford and a Fellow of St Antony's College. His first book was *Lenin and the Russian Revolution.* He is at the moment engaged as co-author with Leonard Schapiro on a study of the origins of Bolshevism.

J.M.Roberts, General Editor of the *Macdonald Library of the 20th Century,* is Fellow and Tutor in Modern History at Merton College, Oxford. He was also General Editor of Purnell's *History of the 20th Century,* and is Joint-Editor of the *English Historical Review* and author of *Europe 1880-1945* in the Longman's History of Europe. He has been English Editor of the Larousse Encyclopedia of Modern History, has reviewed for *The Observer, New Statesman* and *Spectator,* and given talks on the BBC.

Library of the 20th Century

Publisher: John Thompson
Editor: Richard Johnson
Executive Editor: Peter Prince
Designed by: Brian Mayers/ Germano Facetti
Design: Henning Boehlke
Research: Evan Davies

Pictures selected from the following sources:

Herman Axelbank 119 123
Bayerisches Hauptstaatsarchiv Munich 92
British Museum 50
Camera Press 15 26 60 62 91 106 120 128
Eupra Munich 12 22 28 32 74 82 87 102 123
Martin Gilbert 100
Illustrated London News 38 95
Imperial War Museum 42 45 122
Keystone 4 56 80 89 91
William Klein 11
Mansell Collection 64 102
Moro Rome 20
Musée Royal de l'Armée Brussels 105
Novosti cover 1 8 14 15 24 27 30 42 43 46 52 54 56 68 70 79 85 89 91 98 103 105 109 115 116 120 123
Popperfoto 18 26 27 40 90
Radio Times Hulton 90
SCR Library 16 26 36 78 99 112 122
Hans Tasiemka 34
Ullstein 48 66 72